Verdura

Lola Randall, your love of eating vegetables has been the main source of inspiration for this book. Thank you, Sausage. X

Verdura

10 Vegetables
100 Italian Recipes

Theo Randall

Photography by Lizzie Mayson

quadrille

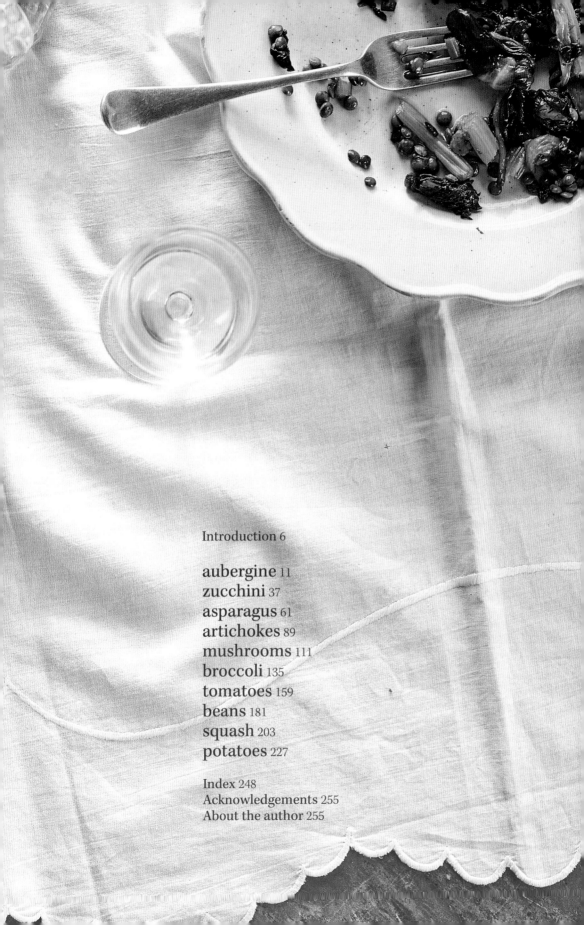

Introduction

My parents have always grown vegetables, especially my father, whose dad was a professional gardener. Peter Randall – a retired architect at 90 years of age – still grows a decent crop of runner beans and a good selection of tomatoes. Having green fingers is a natural skill that is not easily taught and tends to come instinctively to those who are blessed. Sadly, I don't have my family's skills. I can grow the odd basil or parsley plant but even then, I grow them from seedlings rather than from seed. Instead, I took more of a shine to cooking them.

My grandfather's tomatoes are still in my memory; the best I have ever tasted. He kept an immaculate greenhouse and grew 'gardeners' delight'. Though a common variety of tomato, the flavour he achieved was something you should only get in a much hotter climate. The experience of growing up eating delicious tomatoes in season had a big impact on my father; he cannot get through a day without eating a fresh tomato. Thanks to supermarkets and the importation of winter tomatoes from Italy, he is able to enjoy his daily lunch of butterhead lettuce and tomatoes, even in tomato-crop-less months.

As a child I would watch my father eat tomatoes, lettuce and cucumbers with such passion it would make me want to eat them too. My mother did all the cooking when we were little, but my dad would always make the salad dressing and take great interest in what was in the salad. I picked this up from a young age and eventually took over salad duties – he even let me make the salad dressing. I'd caught Delia Smith on the telly tossing a salad with vinaigrette, explaining passionately how important it was to mix the salad with the dressing, and I felt inspired. I became hooked on eating and experimenting with salad. A seed had been planted.

At the ripe old age of 12, I progressed from salad to sandwiches. And at 15 years old I got a job washing dishes at a restaurant called Starr's Bistro. From those humble kitchen beginnings, things took off – I moved to L'Etoile under Keith Starr, and then to Chez Max, working under the guidance of Max Markarian. This was a great learning period for me, and Max was an amazing teacher. After 12 months at Chez Max, I started to become more confident and organized. In those days, vegetables played second fiddle to meat and fish, but Max insisted that the same care had to be taken whether I was cooking lamb or blanching spinach. I now always think of Max when blanching vegetables.

After three and a half years at Chez Max, my culinary hero at that time, Alastair Little, suggested I meet with Rose Gray and Ruth Rogers as they were looking for chefs for their restaurant... I will never forget the moment I walked into The River Café. Rose was sitting at the bar and Ruthie was behind the coffee machine dressed in chef whites. Rose turned to me and said, 'so do you think you are a good cook then?' I was a bit taken aback by her direct approach but answered confidently. Ruthie was much warmer and asked what kind of coffee I would like. We sat down and they showed me a folder of their previous menus and the tattered cookbooks that inspired their cooking. I suddenly felt comfortable – as though I were leafing through my mother's cookbooks at home, squeezed onto messy shelves alongside big jars of macerating fruit. I really felt that this was the place I was supposed to be. We agreed that I would come back the following week to cook for them.

On the trial shift I made a salad of artichoke hearts with green beans, rocket, olive tapenade and parmesan shavings. Sounds simple but it was delicious – and way ahead of the times in 1989.

My first month at The River Café was so exciting, there were so many young, interesting people working at the restaurant and the weather was fantastic, so all the doors were always open, even in the evenings, and all the front of house staff wore whatever they wanted. At the end of busy shifts we would sit by the river with cold beers and discuss what was going to be on the menu next. I loved it and couldn't wait until the next day.

As time passed and the restaurant got busier and busier, so did the menu and the prep. Rose and Ruthie would come back from a weekend in Italy with a bag of seeds or a sack of greens that they had bought that morning in a market. Vegetables were very much the star of the show at The River Café. A simple plate of baked borlotti beans on bruschetta with a delicious olive oil was entirely 'less-is-more' but, importantly, confident. Our plates only got better as more Italian produce started coming into Covent Garden market.

After a couple of years at The River Café, I took some time out and went to work at Chez Panisse in Berkeley, California. Here I was shown how important produce is. I worked in the restaurant downstairs, where we cooked a daily changing 4-course menu every day, except on Sundays. I loved it, the produce was exceptional and came from all over California, but the best we ever got was from a farm called Chino Ranch. They would send these boxes of what they called 'beets', which were actually several varieties of coloured beetroots, turnips and carrots. They were simply washed, cut in half and cooked to order in a little butter, salt and pepper. The flavour was incredible – so pure and natural – I can taste them as I write.

Chez Panisse and its founder, Alice Waters, became responsible for the term 'California cuisine' and I felt very proud to be working there. I remember seeing two guys carrying a huge box into the kitchen one day and all the chefs rushed from their sections to see what was in it. There were lots of 'wows' and 'they look amazing' so I politely squeezed my way to the front of the crowd. There in front of me was the largest quantity of fresh porcini mushrooms I had ever seen. I came to learn this was a regular occurrence at CP, as every day someone local would pop by with incredible foraged produce or carefully grown fruit and vegetables from their garden or farm and try to sell them to the restaurant. I guess if it was good enough for Chez Panisse then all the neighbouring restaurants would want some too.

I loved my time in California, but eventually it was time to come back to London and back to The River Café. I was completely inspired on my return and was excited to be back cooking in the kitchen I called home. Over the years, The River Café grew and so did the team. Looking back, those early moments in that special kitchen were so new and exciting for me personally, but it's also clear to me now how revolutionary the cooking there was, through its celebration of fruits and vegetables.

Today we are spoilt for choice with an abundance of wonderful produce at our fingertips, but we should still treat it with the respect it deserves. I've tried to convey that through these pages. Italian food at its core is very much vegetable based, and the Italians have perfected the art of getting a huge amount of flavour out of just a handful of good-quality ingredients. A simple pasta dish with some fried courgettes or sautéed wild mushrooms is a feast in itself.

As ever, always try to buy vegetables that are in season, as they will be at their best in flavour and price. So, the next time you are shopping and you see a good-looking aubergine or handsome tomato, perhaps pop it in your basket and cook a recipe from this book? **TR**.

Please note: In some recipes I have suggested cheeses that are not traditionally vegetarian – namely parmesan, pecorino, fontina, taleggio and scamorza. If needed, please use commonly available vegetarian alternatives instead.

AUBERGINE

Aubergine polpette with fennel salad

Serves 4

4 medium aubergines
  (eggplants)
1 egg
1 garlic clove, crushed to
  a paste with a little sea salt
1 tbsp chopped flat-leaf
  parsley
150g (5½oz) breadcrumbs
150g (5½oz) parmesan,
  finely grated
200ml (7fl oz) sunflower oil
sea salt and freshly ground
  black pepper

To coat
100g (3½oz) plain
  (all-purpose) flour
1 egg, beaten
100g (3½oz) breadcrumbs

For the salad
2 fennel bulbs
1 tbsp red wine vinegar
2 tbsp extra-virgin olive oil
1 shallot, finely chopped
2 tbsp miniature capers in
  vinegar, drained
4 flat-leaf parsley sprigs,
  leaves picked

I love a croquette, and there aren't many better than aubergine polpette. The smooth, creamy texture of the aubergine on the inside combined with the crispy outer is delicious. The crunchy fennel salad dotted with salty capers is perfect at counteracting the richness of the dish.

Preheat the oven to 200°C/180°C fan/400°F/Gas 6.

Place the aubergines on a roasting tray and prick them all over with a fork. Bake in the oven for 1 hour until completely soft on the inside. Leave to cool for 20 minutes, then cut them in half lengthways and scoop out the soft, cooked flesh, removing as much skin as you can. Finely chop the flesh, then place it in a fine sieve to drain the excess liquid.

In a large bowl, beat the egg, then add the drained, cooked aubergine flesh, the crushed garlic in salt, chopped parsley, breadcrumbs, parmesan and some black pepper. Mix well.

Take out 3 lipped plates or shallow bowls and place the flour on one, the beaten egg on another and the breadcrumbs on the last.

Using a tablespoon, scoop some of the aubergine mixture and roll it into a ball about the size of a golf ball. Then with one hand, roll the aubergine ball in the flour, then the beaten egg and finally in the breadcrumbs. Repeat with the remaining aubergine mixture.

In a small saucepan, heat the sunflower oil to a medium heat, then add the coated aubergine balls in batches to the hot oil, no more than 4 at a time. Cook for 4 minutes, turning occasionally, until golden brown on all sides, then remove with a slotted spoon and place on a wire rack. Keep them warm on an oven tray in an oven preheated to 150°C/130°C fan/300°F/Gas 2.

To make the salad, use a mandoline or sharp knife to cut the fennel into very thin slices, then place in a bowl with some ice and water. Leave for 10 minutes so the fennel goes really crisp. Drain and spin in a salad spinner until dry.

Add the vinegar, olive oil, shallot, capers and parsley leaves to a bowl, then add the fennel. Season with salt and black pepper and toss well. Serve with the warm polpette.

Aubergine stuffed with orzo, zucchini and tomatoes

Serves 4

4 large aubergines (eggplants)
3 tbsp extra-virgin olive oil,
  plus extra for greasing
6 medium courgettes
  (zucchini), sliced into 1cm
  (½in) rounds
1 garlic clove, finely sliced
6 basil leaves
250g (9oz) dried orzo pasta
1 mild red chilli, deseeded
  and finely chopped
200g (7oz) cherry tomatoes,
  quartered
250g (9oz) smoked scamorza,
  grated
sea salt and freshly ground
  black pepper

A couple of summers ago we went to Ibiza with a group of friends. We had great food, as one of the group had done some serious restaurant research beforehand. Out of all the dishes we ate, a simple baked aubergine was one of my favourites. I loved the way the aubergine's texture was so much part of the dish, and the cheese on top (they used tetilla) had a lovely creamy taste. This is my version. I have used smoked scamorza, as I find it brings out the flavours of the aubergine more. If you have a BBQ, try cooking the whole aubergines on it for a really authentic smoky flavour.

Preheat the oven to 200°C/180°C fan/400°F/Gas 6. Line a baking sheet with foil and rub a little olive oil over it.

With a fork, prick the aubergines all over and place them on the prepared baking sheet. Bake in the oven for 1 hour, turning each aubergine over after 30 minutes so they cook evenly.

Remove from the oven and leave to cool down on the baking sheet. Turn the oven down to 180°C/160°C fan/350°F/Gas 4. When cool enough to handle, take a sharp knife and score down the middle of each aubergine, about a third of the way through the flesh. Now pull open the flesh on each so you have 4 butterflied aubergines. Leave to one side.

Heat the olive oil in a non-stick frying pan that has a lid, then add the courgettes, garlic and a good pinch of salt. Cook, stirring frequently, for 5 minutes, then place the lid on top, turn down the heat and cook for a further 15 minutes. Add the basil leaves, season well and leave to one side.

Cook the orzo in a pan of boiling salted water for 2 minutes less than the packet suggests. Drain into a sieve and mix in a little olive oil. Place the orzo in a large bowl and add the cooked courgettes, chilli and tomatoes, seasoning with salt and black pepper. Spoon the mixture onto the open aubergines, making sure the aubergines are covered with the mixture.

Cover each aubergine with the grated smoked scamorza and place back in the oven for 15 minutes until the cheese is melted and golden in places. Serve immediately.

Mezze maniche with slow-cooked aubergines

Serves 4

3 medium aubergines
(eggplants)
6 tbsp extra-virgin olive oil
500g (1lb 2oz) dried mezze
maniche pasta
1 garlic clove, finely sliced
2 mild green chillies,
deseeded and finely
chopped
2 tbsp miniature capers in
vinegar, drained
2 tbsp finely chopped
flat-leaf parsley
100g (3½oz) ricotta salata
or feta, grated
sea salt and freshly ground
black pepper

**Mezze maniche means 'half sleeves' and these little pasta
tubes have deep ridges that hold any sauce very well.
Adding the roasted aubergine to the pasta last-minute
ensures you have all the flavour of the aubergine but retain
its unmistakable texture. Ricotta salata is salted ricotta
(low in fat but very high in flavour) so be careful how much
salt you add to the dish while cooking. If you can't get hold
of ricotta salata, feta is a good substitute.**

Preheat the oven to 180°C/160°C fan/350°F/Gas 4.

Cut the stems off the top of the aubergines and cut each
lengthways into quarters, then across into 2cm (³⁄₄in) slices.
Add 4 tablespoons of the olive oil to a large bowl, then mix in
the aubergines thoroughly so that each piece is coated in oil.

Line a roasting tray with baking paper and scatter the oiled
aubergine pieces onto it in a single layer. If your tray is not big
enough, divide the aubergines between 2 trays. Cook in the oven
for 25 minutes, until soft all the way through. Remove and leave
to cool.

Cook the mezze maniche in a pan of boiling salted water for
3 minutes less than the packet suggests.

While the pasta is cooking, heat a large frying pan over a medium
heat, add the remaining 2 tablespoons of olive oil, the garlic,
chillies, capers and parsley and cook for a couple of minutes.

Using a slotted spoon or sieve, remove the mezze maniche from
the cooking water and add to the frying pan. Add 2 ladlefuls
of the pasta cooking water and cook over a medium heat for a
couple of minutes, stirring and tossing the pasta from time to
time. Add the roasted aubergine and give the pan a good stir
or toss, so all the cooked aubergine is combined with the pasta,
then cook for a further minute or two. Check the seasoning then
serve in warm pasta bowls with the grated ricotta salata on top.

Tomato and aubergine risotto

Serves 4

3 medium aubergines
  (eggplants)
8 tbsp extra-virgin olive oil
1 garlic clove, finely sliced
8 basil leaves
400ml (14fl oz) tomato passata
  (strained tomatoes)
2 celery stalks, finely chopped
1 small onion, finely chopped
250g (9oz) Carnaroli
  risotto rice
75ml (2¼fl oz) dry white wine
75g (2½oz) butter
150g (5½oz) parmesan,
  grated, plus extra to serve
sea salt and freshly ground
  black pepper

For the vegetable stock
1 medium leek, cut into 2cm
  (¾in) pieces
3 carrots, peeled and cut into
  2cm (¾in) pieces
2 celery stalks
a few flat-leaf parsley stalks
2 fresh thyme sprigs
  (not lemon thyme)
1 tsp sea salt
2 litres (68fl oz) water

Risotto with aubergines my not sound very classically Italian but in Sicily you find this very popular combination in many forms. The term 'alla Norma' is often used to describe pasta dishes, but it applies here too; a simple but delicious combination of tomato and aubergine. Any leftover risotto makes great arancini... very Sicilian!

Place all the stock ingredients in a large saucepan and cook for 45 minutes over a high heat. Strain through a sieve, discarding the vegetables and keeping the stock. When ready to cook the risotto, place the stock over a low heat and keep it hot.

Meanwhile, preheat the oven to 180°C/160°C fan/350°F/Gas 4.

Cut the stems off the top of the aubergines and cut each lengthways into quarters, then across into 2cm (¾in) slices. Add 4 tablespoons of the olive oil to a large bowl, then mix in the aubergines thoroughly so that each piece is coated in oil.

Line a roasting tray with baking paper and scatter the oiled aubergine pieces onto it in a single layer. If your tray is not big enough, divide the aubergines between 2 trays. Cook in the oven for 25 minutes, until soft all the way through. Remove and leave to cool.

While the aubergines are roasting, add 2 tablespoons of the olive oil to a hot, large frying pan, then add the garlic and half of the basil leaves and cook gently for 1 minute before adding the passata. Cook until the passata has reduced by half, season with salt and black pepper and remove from the heat.

Add the remaining 2 tablespoons of olive oil to a hot, large, straight-sided saucepan, then add the celery and onion. Cook for 3 minutes, then add the rice and cook for a further 3 minutes so the rice absorbs the olive oil and goes translucent. Add the wine and cook until absorbed, then start adding the hot vegetable stock, a ladleful at a time, so the rice is always just covered. Keep doing this for 10 minutes over a medium heat so the rice is bubbling away. Next, stir in the tomato sauce, then keep adding the stock, cooking for a further 5 minutes before stirring through the remaining basil, the butter and parmesan.

Add the cooked aubergines, turn down the heat and check the seasoning. Give the risotto a good final stir, so all the ingredients are nicely emulsified. Serve in warm pasta bowls with extra parmesan on top.

Aubergine, red pepper and chickpea stew

Serves 4

3 medium aubergines
  (eggplants)
7 tbsp extra-virgin olive oil,
  plus extra to finish
1 garlic clove, finely sliced
1 medium red onion,
  finely chopped
1 mild red chilli, deseeded
  and finely chopped
4 celery stalks, finely chopped
3 red (bell) peppers,
  deseeded and cut into
  roughly 2cm (¾in) pieces
4 medium potatoes (Cyprus
  or Désirée are best), cut
  into 2cm (¾in) pieces
300ml (10fl oz) tomato passata
  (strained tomatoes)
1 tsp chopped fresh oregano
1 x 400g (14oz) can of
  chickpeas, drained
  and rinsed
200ml (7fl oz) boiling water
150ml (5fl oz) sour cream
sea salt and freshly ground
  black pepper

For the gremolata
zest of 1 lemon
2 tbsp chopped flat-leaf
  parsley
1 garlic clove, crushed to
  a paste with a little sea salt

This is a quick and easy vegetable stew, perfect for a midweek dinner. I have included gremolata, as I think it is a great addition: the lemon zest, garlic and parsley give the stew an extra flavour and lift the dish to new heights.

Mix all the gremolata ingredients together and leave to one side.

Preheat the oven to 180°C/160°C fan/350°F/Gas 4.

Cut the stems off the top of the aubergines and cut each lengthways into quarters, then across into 2cm (¾in) slices. Add 4 tablespoons of the olive oil to a large bowl, then mix in the aubergines thoroughly so that each piece is coated in oil.

Line a roasting tray with baking paper and scatter the aubergine pieces onto it in a single layer. If your tray is not big enough, divide the aubergines between 2 trays. Cook in the oven for 25 minutes until soft all the way through.

Add the remaining 3 tablespoons of olive oil to a hot, large saucepan that has a tight-fitting lid, then add the garlic, onion, chilli and celery and cook over a medium heat for 5 minutes. Add the red peppers, potatoes and ½ teaspoon of sea salt, place the lid on top and cook over a low heat for 20 minutes. Now add the tomato passata, oregano, chickpeas and boiling water. Cook slowly for a further 15 minutes, with the lid askew so some moisture can evaporate.

Add the cooked aubergines to the vegetable and chickpea stew, stirring well so all the ingredients are nicely combined. Transfer the stew to a large, warm serving dish. Finish off with some spoonfuls of sour cream, a drizzle of olive oil and plenty of gremolata sprinkled on top.

Aubergine and smoked scamorza 'Milanese' with salsa pizzaiola

Serves 4

2 large aubergines (eggplants)
4 tbsp extra-virgin olive oil
250g (9oz) smoked scamorza,
  cut into 8 thin slices
100g (3½oz) plain
  (all-purpose) flour
100g (3½oz) breadcrumbs
2 eggs, beaten
100ml (3½fl oz) sunflower oil,
  for shallow-frying
sea salt and freshly ground
  black pepper

For the salsa pizzaiola
2 tbsp extra-virgin olive oil
1 garlic clove, finely sliced
10 pitted taggiasche olives,
  chopped
1 tsp chopped fresh oregano
300ml (10fl oz) tomato passata
  (strained tomatoes)

For the braised greens
250g (9oz) kale leaves
500g (1lb 2oz) spinach
100g (3½oz) wild rocket
  (arugula)
2 tbsp extra-virgin olive oil
1 garlic clove, finely sliced
½ tsp crushed fennel seeds

This is as meaty as you can get without any meat. The texture of the fried, breadcrumbed aubergines with the smoked scamorza is so tasty, and also filling. The pizzaiola is a great sauce to serve with almost anything, as it is seasoned with oregano, garlic and olives. I have used taggiasche olives here, but if you can't find these then niçoise are a good alternative.

Preheat the oven to 180°C/160°C fan/350°F/Gas 4 and line 2 roasting trays with baking paper.

Make the salsa pizzaiola. Add the olive oil to a hot, medium-sized saucepan, then add the garlic, olives and oregano. Cook gently for 1 minute, then add the passata and cook over a low heat until the sauce has reduced by half, about 10 minutes. Season with salt and black pepper and remove from the heat.

Cut the stem off each aubergine and cut lengthways into 4 even slices, so you have 8 long slices in total. Add 2 tablespoons of olive oil to each of the lined trays, then place 4 aubergine slices on each. Cook in the oven for 25 minutes, carefully turning each slice after 10 minutes, so the aubergine cooks evenly and is covered in the oil. Remove from the oven and leave to cool.

Meanwhile, make the braised greens. In a pan of boiling salted water, blanch the kale for 4 minutes, then, using a slotted spoon, transfer the kale to a large colander. Blanch the spinach in the boiling water for 1 minute, then take out with a slotted spoon and place on top of the kale. Finally, blanch the rocket for 2 minutes, take out with a slotted spoon and add to the spinach and kale in the colander. Discard the blanching water and wipe the pan clean, then place back over a medium heat. Squeeze out the excess water from the greens then roughly chop them.

Add the olive oil to the hot saucepan, then add the garlic and crushed fennel seeds. Cook gently for 1 minute, then add the chopped greens back to the pan and cook for 2 minutes. Season with salt and pepper, remove from the heat and set aside.

Once the cooked aubergine has cooled down, place 2 slices of smoked scamorza on top of 4 of the aubergine slices, then take the remaining 4 aubergine slices and place them on top of the smoked scamorza, gently pushing down to make an aubergine and scamorza sandwich.

Continued overleaf

Aubergine and smoked scamorza 'Milanese' with salsa pizzaiola
continued

Take 3 lipped plates or shallow bowls and place the flour on one, the breadcrumbs on another and the beaten eggs on the third. Have ready a flat tray to place the breaded aubergines on.

Carefully lift up an aubergine and scamorza sandwich and place it in the flour, coating both sides and the edges. Next, coat in the beaten egg, and finally in the breadcrumbs. It's important that it is completely covered on both sides and the edges, so the layers stay together when fried. Repeat with the other 3 sandwiches.

Heat the sunflower oil in a large non-stick frying pan over a medium heat. Test it's hot enough by adding a breadcrumb; if it sizzles but doesn't go brown too quickly, the oil is ready. It's important the oil is not too hot or the breadcrumbs will colour too quickly before the aubergine and scamorza cook together (the aubergine is already cooked but the scamorza has to melt inside so it becomes soft and creamy).

Add a coated aubergine sandwich to the hot oil (cook them one at a time) and fry for 3 minutes, then carefully flip it and cook on the other side for 3 minutes, so each side is nicely golden. Once cooked, place on a wire rack with an ovenproof tray underneath to catch any excess oil (do not place on kitchen paper or they will turn soggy).

Once they are all cooked and draining on the wire rack, place the rack and tray in the oven at 160°C/140°C fan/320°F/Gas 3 for 3 minutes.

Divide the braised greens between large, warmed dinner plates in a mound to one side of the plate, then take a hot aubergine 'Milanese' and place it on the other side of the plate. Spoon a good dollop of the salsa pizzaiola over the aubergine. Enjoy!

Aubergine, kale and sweet onion frittata

Serves 4

9 tbsp extra-virgin olive oil
1 garlic clove, finely sliced
1 tsp thyme leaves
  (not lemon thyme)
2 medium onions, finely sliced
2 medium aubergines
  (eggplants)
250g (9oz) kale leaves
6 eggs
1 tsp chopped flat-leaf parsley
150g (5½oz) parmesan,
  grated
sea salt and freshly ground
  black pepper

As you may know, I love a frittata. They are simple to make and can feed a lot of hungry people quickly, with little fuss, and without needing lots of pots and pans. Kale is a more cost-effective alternative to chard and spinach and comes in many forms. In supermarkets you'll often find it shredded and bagged, which is fine, but make sure you remove the stems as they can be very stringy. It can be fiddly but the end result will be much better.

Preheat the oven to 180°C/160°C fan/350°F/Gas 4.

Add 3 tablespoons of the olive oil to a hot, large, non-stick frying pan, then add the garlic, thyme and onions. Add a good pinch of salt and cook gently over a low heat for 15 minutes until the onions are soft. Remove from the heat and leave to cool.

While the onions are cooking, cut the stems off the top of the aubergines and cut each lengthways into quarters, then across into 2cm (¾in) slices. Add 4 tablespoons of the olive oil to a large bowl, then mix in the aubergines thoroughly so that each piece is coated in oil.

Line a roasting tray with baking paper and scatter the oiled aubergine pieces onto it in a single layer. If your tray is not big enough, divide the aubergines between 2 trays. Cook in the oven for 25 minutes, until soft all the way through. Remove and leave to cool, but leave the oven on.

Cook the kale leaves in a pan of boiling salted water for 4 minutes, until tender (undercooked kale tends to be a bit tough, so check it's properly done). Drain the kale in a colander and squeeze out any excess water. Roughly chop and leave to one side.

In a large bowl, beat the eggs well, then add the cooked onions, chopped kale, roasted aubergines, parsley and parmesan. Mix well and season with salt and black pepper.

Continued overleaf

Aubergine, kale and sweet onion frittata
continued

Take the large non-stick frying pan you used to cook the onions, give it a wipe, then add the remaining 2 tablespoons of olive oil. Place over a medium heat and, when hot, move the pan around so the oil covers all the sides of the pan. Add the egg and aubergine mixture to the pan in an even layer and cook over a low heat for 3 minutes so the frittata starts to set. Transfer to the oven and cook for 5 minutes or until set; if your pan has a plastic handle, don't worry about putting it in the oven, as heatproof plastic handles won't melt at this temperature. Check the frittata is set by giving the pan a wiggle, then remove from the oven.

Take a chopping board and place it on top of the frying pan. Holding the handle of the pan tightly with a cloth, and with your other hand firmly on top of the chopping board, confidently turn out the frittata onto the chopping board.

Serve warm with a mixed leaf salad or, once cold, cut into bite-sized pieces and serve as a canapé for a party.

Panzerotti stuffed with aubergine, tomato and mozzarella

Makes 18

4 medium aubergines
  (eggplants)
4 tbsp extra-virgin olive oil
500g (1lb 2oz) cow's milk
  mozzarella, cut into 18 slices
18 basil leaves
200ml (7fl oz) sunflower oil
sea salt and freshly ground
  black pepper

For the panzerotti dough
15g (½oz) fresh yeast or
  7g (¼oz) dried yeast
600ml (20fl oz) warm water
5g (⅛oz) caster (superfine)
  sugar
2 tbsp extra-virgin olive oil
500g (1lb 2oz) strong white
  bread flour, plus extra
  for dusting
500g (1lb 2oz) tipo 00 flour
10g (½oz) fine sea salt

For the tomato sauce
3 tbsp extra-virgin olive oil
1 garlic clove, thinly sliced
6 basil leaves
600ml (20fl oz) tomato passata
  (strained tomatoes)

I first had panzerotti in the town of Ostuni in a very smart restaurant called Aqua Sale, which at the time was a favourite of ours as the food was so good. We ordered the *antipasti del giorno*, which was usually an amazing selection of small dishes, but on this occasion lots of beautiful fish and shellfish arrived – to my, Max's and Natalie's delight; but little Lola was not so happy as she doesn't like fish. She didn't eat much the whole dinner and was not pleased with the empty shells and remaining bones left on the table after our main course of whole roasted orata and Gallipoli red prawns.

Anyway, she wasn't that bothered, as one of the reasons we had chosen the restaurant was because they had the best view of the fireworks from their roof terrace. It was the last day of the Cavalcata di Sant'Oronzo, when each town in the region of Puglia tries to outdo each other on the size of their fireworks display. As we took our seats on the terrace, a young waiter walked around offering panzerotti. Lola took one look at the tomato and mozzarella fried pastries and grabbed one. I will never forget the look of enjoyment on her little face as she gobbled up two in quick succession. The fireworks were pretty good, too.

Mix the yeast with the warm water, sugar and olive oil in a medium bowl, stirring so all the ingredients are mixed well.

Place the flours and salt in the bowl of a stand mixture and pour in the yeasted water. With the dough hook attached, mix for 10 minutes so the dough becomes elastic. Take the dough out of the bowl, place it on a chopping board and divide into 18 even-sized pieces.

Roll each piece into a ball and place on a tray dusted with flour to prevent them from sticking. Cover the tray with cling film (plastic wrap) and place somewhere warm for 1 hour, to allow the dough to rise.

Preheat the oven to 180°C/160°C fan/350°F/Gas 4.

While the dough is rising, make the tomato sauce. Add the olive oil to a hot, large frying pan, then add the garlic and basil leaves. Cook for 1 minute over a low heat, then add the passata and a good pinch of salt. Cook until the passata has reduced by half, then set aside to cool.

Meanwhile, cut the stems off the top of the aubergines and cut each lengthways into quarters, then across into 2cm (¾in) slices. Add the olive oil to a large bowl, then mix in the aubergines thoroughly so that each piece is coated in oil.

Line a roasting tray with baking paper and scatter the oiled aubergine pieces onto it in a single layer. If your tray is not big enough, divide the aubergines between 2 trays. Cook in the oven for 25 minutes, until soft all the way through. Remove and leave to cool.

Once the dough has risen, roll the dough balls out into 18 discs about 15cm (6in) in diameter. Place a spoonful of tomato sauce in the middle of each disc, then 5 pieces of roasted aubergine, a generous slice of mozzarella and a basil leaf. Using a pastry brush with some water on it, brush the inside edge of each dough disc; this will help the dough stick and will prevent it opening when shallow-frying. Push the edges together tightly, so you have a half-moon shape, and crimp the edges together as you would for a pie (see photos overleaf as a guide). Repeat this until you have shaped all the panzerotti.

Heat the sunflower oil in a large non-stick frying pan and gently fry the panzerotti, in batches, for 3 minutes on each side. Remove from the pan carefully and place on a wire rack. Serve after a couple of minutes, wrapped in some kitchen paper. This is southern Italian street food at its best and tastes better eaten standing up!

Pictured overleaf

Aubergines, red peppers and tomatoes with chopped burrata

Serves 4

4 medium aubergines
  (eggplants)
5 tbsp extra-virgin olive oil,
  plus extra for drizzling
1 medium onion, sliced
1 garlic clove, sliced, plus
  an extra peeled clove
  for rubbing
4 red (bell) peppers,
  deseeded and cut into
  roughly 2cm (¾in) pieces
600ml (20fl oz) tomato passata
  (strained tomatoes)
8 basil leaves, torn
1 ciabatta loaf
150g (5½oz) burrata
sea salt and freshly ground
  black pepper

There is something really comforting about the combination of slow-cooked aubergines, peppers and tomatoes. I love the meatiness of an aubergine, and adding chopped burrata makes the flavours and textures of the slow-cooked vegetables really stand out. Ciabatta is a favourite bread of mine and toasting it a for a few minutes makes it the perfect accompaniment to this dish. This is one of those recipes you can enjoy all year round.

Preheat the oven to 180°C/160°C fan/350°F/Gas 4.

Slice the aubergines widthways into discs 2cm (¾in) thick, then cut each disc in half, so you have half-moons. Place in a large bowl with a sprinkling of salt and 3 tablespoons of the olive oil. Mix thoroughly so the aubergine pieces are coated in oil, then place the slices on a baking sheet lined with baking paper, in a single layer that fills the tray.

Cook in the oven for 15 minutes, then flip the aubergine slices over. Put back in the oven for a further 10 minutes, then check they are cooked by pushing a sharp knife into the outside edge of an aubergine slice; if the knife goes through easily and there is no resistance, then it is cooked. Remove from the oven, but keep the oven on.

Add the remaining 2 tablespoons of olive oil to a hot large, heavy-based saucepan, then add the onion and sliced garlic and cook for 10 minutes over a low heat. Add the peppers to the onions with a generous pinch of salt. Place a tight-fitting lid on the pan so the peppers start to steam and become softer. After 10 minutes, add the passata and cook over a low heat for a further 10 minutes until the passata has reduced by half. Add the torn basil and roasted aubergines, mix well and leave to cook very gently for a further 5 minutes so the aubergines mingle with the peppers, tomatoes and basil. Add salt and black pepper to taste, remove from the heat and set aside.

Cut the ciabatta in half lengthways and place in the hot oven for 5 minutes. Remove and rub both ciabatta halves with a little garlic, then add a drizzle of olive oil. Cut into 3cm (1¼in) pieces.

Drain the burrata of any excess liquid and chop finely.

Place the cooked aubergines, peppers and tomatoes in a nice serving dish and spoon over the chopped burrata. Serve with the roasted ciabatta in the middle of the table for everyone to help themselves.

Grilled marinated aubergines with chilli and mint

Serves 4 as a simple starter or side dish

4 medium aubergines
(eggplants)
1 garlic clove, crushed to a
paste with a little sea salt
1 tbsp red wine vinegar
2 mild red chillies, deseeded
and finely chopped
3 tbsp extra-virgin olive oil
6 mint leaves
100g (3½oz) wild rocket
(arugula)
50g (1¾oz) ricotta salata
or feta

Cooking aubergines in a griddle pan takes patience but is worth it – try to achieve perfect criss-cross marks on both sides if possible. This is also a perfect dish to cook on the BBQ. The dressing of red chilli, garlic, mint and vinegar cuts wonderfully through the flavour of the smoky aubergines.

You can also make this into a very tasty canapé. Roll up the grilled aubergines with grated ricotta salata in the middle, then place a toothpick through the centre to hold it in place. Serve with the sauce drizzled on top.

Heat a griddle pan until very hot.

Slice the aubergines into slices or rounds 1cm (½in) thick, and carefully place on the hot griddle pan. Make sure you don't overcrowd the pan, so each slice can cook evenly. After a couple of minutes, the aubergines should have some dark griddle marks. Turn each slice clockwise on the griddle pan so you keep cooking on the same side but you don't get too much char in the same place. Cook for 2 more minutes, then flip the slices over. You should have lovely pronounced criss-cross marks on the top side. Repeat this cooking method for the other side. It is very important to cook aubergines all the way through as they taste strange when not cooked properly, so ensure they are soft before removing them from the pan. Place on a wire rack to cool.

In a large bowl, add the crushed garlic in salt, the vinegar, chillies and olive oil. Add the grilled aubergines and mix so all the ingredients coat the aubergines. Place on a nice flat serving plate or platter.

In the same bowl you mixed the aubergines in, add the mint leaves and rocket and mix with the remnants of the marinade. Place the leaves on top of the marinated aubergines. Using a grater, shave the ricotta salata all over the rocket and mint.

ZUCCHINI

Baked eggs with zucchini and spinach

Serves 4

2 tbsp extra-virgin olive oil,
plus extra for greasing and
drizzling
2 medium courgettes
(zucchini), sliced into 1cm
(½in) rounds
1 garlic clove, finely sliced,
plus an extra peeled clove
for rubbing
400g (14oz) spinach,
blanched, squeezed of
excess water, then chopped
8 eggs
4 tbsp crème fraîche
4 tsp sun-dried tomato paste
1 tsp dried oregano
1 ciabatta loaf
sea salt and freshly ground
black pepper

**I love baked eggs – when we were little my dad would
always make us *oeufs cocotte* on Sunday mornings. He was
very precise and would take his time buttering the dishes,
sprinkling dried oregano and then breaking the eggs one
by one into the cocottes. They were finished off with fresh
chopped chives; I can almost taste them as I write this.**

**Here is a more brunch-style version of my dad's eggs.
The toasted ciabatta is a must, so you can scoop everything
up and dip into the eggs.**

Preheat the oven to 180°C/160°C fan/350°F/Gas 4.

Add the olive oil to a hot non-stick frying pan that has a lid,
then add the courgettes and garlic. Add a pinch of salt and stir
the courgettes. Place the lid on top and cook for 10 minutes,
then take off the lid and cook for a further 5 minutes or until the
courgettes are soft and have a little colour.

Rub the inside of a baking dish with olive oil, scatter in the
cooked, chopped spinach, then top with the cooked courgettes.
Season well with salt and pepper. Break the eggs evenly over
the top, then dollop with the crème fraîche and sun-dried tomato
paste. Sprinkle with the oregano and season again.

Alternatively, to make individual portions, grease 4 ramekins with
olive oil. Layer as above, adding two eggs to each ramekin along
with 1 tablespoon of crème fraîche, 1 teaspoon of sun-dried
tomato paste and ¼ teaspoon of oregano per portion.

Place the baking dish or ramekins in a roasting tin. Boil a kettle
and pour the just-boiled water into the roasting tin so it comes
halfway up the sides of the dish(es).

Bake in the oven for 10 minutes until the eggs are set, then serve
immediately with some toasted ciabatta that has been rubbed
with garlic and drizzled with a little olive oil. (If using ramekins,
I find a fish slice helpful to lift them out of the hot water.)

Zucchini, fennel and radish salad with walnuts and pecorino

**Serves 4 as a starter
or side dish**

4 medium courgettes
  (zucchini)
1 large fennel bulb
8 red radishes
1 tub of mustard cress
150g (5½oz) walnuts
150g (5½oz) pecorino,
  finely shaved

For the dressing
1 shallot, finely sliced
1 tbsp white balsamic vinegar
1 tbsp Dijon mustard
juice of 1 lemon
1 tbsp honey
5 tbsp extra-virgin olive oil
sea salt and freshly ground
  black pepper

**I love making this salad, especially when it's warm outside.
Try to choose young, firm courgettes as they will taste much
nicer and have a better texture than large, watery ones. The
honey mustard dressing adds lots of flavour and, finished off
with the crunch of walnuts and saltiness of pecorino, makes
for a simple but very tasty salad.**

First make the dressing. Add the shallot, balsamic vinegar and
a pinch each of salt and black pepper to a large bowl. Leave to
marinate for 10 minutes, then add the mustard, lemon juice and
honey. Stir together, then add the olive oil slowly, stirring so the
dressing emulsifies. Leave to one side.

Wash and trim the courgettes, fennel and radishes, reserving
the fennel's green fronds. Using a mandoline, finely slice
the courgettes into long ribbons and the fennel bulb and the
radishes into rounds (use a sharp knife if you are not confident
doing them on a mandoline). Place all the prepared vegetables
on a tea (dish) towel to absorb any excess water. Snip off the
mustard cress.

Add the courgette, fennel, radish and cress to the dressing and
toss thoroughly so that the vegetables are nicely coated in the
dressing. Scatter with the walnuts and pecorino, then tear and
sprinkle over the reserved fennel fronds. Serve immediately.

Zucchini scapece

Serves 6 as a snack

8 medium courgettes
  (zucchini)
500ml (17fl oz) sunflower oil
1 garlic clove, crushed to a
  paste with a little sea salt
2 red chillies, deseeded and
  finely chopped
10 mint leaves, finely chopped
2 tbsp red wine vinegar
sea salt

These fried courgette slices are probably the best pre-dinner snack you could make. The key to getting them crispy is to use the freshest courgettes and dry them thoroughly after salting and washing them. Taking your time helps too; if you have an electric deep-fat fryer, cook the courgettes in small batches in clean sunflower oil.

The chilli, garlic, mint and vinegar really bring the courgettes to life. I guarantee there will not be any leftovers.

Using a mandoline or slicing attachment on a food processor, cut the courgettes in 5mm (¼in) rounds. Place on a large tray and sprinkle 2 teaspoons of salt over them. This will draw out the excess water. Leave the salt on them for 10 minutes, then place the salted courgettes in a large colander and give them a good rinse in cold water. Once they are rinsed, take 2 tea (dish) towels and scatter the courgettes all over each towel. Roll them up and press firmly so the excess water is absorbed by the towels.

Add the sunflower oil to a large frying pan and set over a medium heat. When the oil is hot, carefully fry the courgettes in batches until they are a light golden brown and crispy. Place the fried courgette slices on a wire rack with a tray underneath to catch any excess oil. Repeat until you have cooked all the courgette slices.

Add the crushed garlic in salt, the chilli, mint and vinegar to a large bowl. Stir together, then add the fried courgette slices. Mix well and place on a large plate in the middle of the table. These are the ultimate pre-lunch/dinner snack.

Yellow zucchini, spring onion, fennel and lentil soup

Serves 4

3 tbsp extra-virgin olive oil,
  plus extra to finish
300g (10½oz) spring onions
  (scallions), finely sliced
1kg (2lb 3oz) yellow
  courgettes (zucchini), sliced
  into 1cm (½in) rounds, then
  in half into half-moons
2 fennel bulbs, cut into 5mm
  (¼in) pieces
1 garlic clove, finely sliced
1 green chilli, deseeded and
  finely chopped
150g (5½oz) dried Umbrian
  or Puy (French) lentils
1 litre (34fl oz) water
200g (7oz) baby spinach
  leaves, washed
1 tbsp chopped flat-leaf
  parsley
200ml (7fl oz) crème fraîche
sea salt and freshly ground
  black pepper

You don't have to use yellow courgettes for this recipe but they tend to be sweeter. If you have courgettes growing in your garden and there are some courgette flowers, add these torn up at the end; their flavour isn't that strong but the texture is great and they look lovely in the soup. If it's very hot outside, this is also delicious served chilled with a drizzle of extra-virgin olive oil on top.

Add the oil to a hot, large, heavy-based saucepan, then add the spring onions, courgettes, fennel, garlic, chilli and 1 teaspoon of salt. Place a lid on the pan and cook over a low heat for 30 minutes, stirring every 5 minutes.

Meanwhile, place the lentils in a separate saucepan and add the water. Cook for 25 minutes until tender, then remove from the heat, leaving the lentils in the cooking water.

Take the lid off the vegetable pan, turn the heat up and cook for 10 minutes so the vegetables start to lightly caramelize. When they have a little colour and have reduced significantly in volume, add the cooked lentils with their cooking liquid.

Bring to a simmer and add the spinach leaves. Cook for a couple of minutes so the leaves wilt, then add the parsley and crème fraîche and cook over a low heat for 10 minutes. Take out a cupful of the soup and blend to a smooth consistency with a stick blender. Return the cup of puréed soup to the pan, add some black pepper and check if the soup needs more salt. Give it a good stir and serve in warm soup bowls with a drizzle of olive oil on top.

Rigatoni with zucchini, mascarpone and pecorino

Serves 4

3 tbsp extra-virgin olive oil
1 garlic clove, finely sliced
2 large shallots, finely sliced
5 medium courgettes
   (zucchini), sliced into 1cm
   (½in) rounds
8 basil leaves
100g (3½oz) mascarpone
500g (1lb 2oz) dried rigatoni
100g (3½oz) pecorino,
   finely grated
sea salt and freshly ground
   black pepper

Slow-cooked courgettes are a family favourite in our house, especially with Lola, who could eat them every day. The difference in flavour by cooking them that little longer, so they slightly caramelize, is extraordinary. Any courgette will do but the smaller, firmer ones have the most flavour. Always add a good pinch of salt to the pan, as this will extract the water in the courgettes and at the same time season them nicely. A simple pasta dish, but one with lots of flavour.

Add the oil to a hot, large, non-stick frying pan that has a lid, then add the garlic and shallots and cook for 30 seconds before adding the courgettes and a good pinch of salt. Cook over a medium heat until the courgettes and shallots get a little bit of colour. Place the lid on top and cook slowly for 20 minutes; the courgettes will become very soft and creamy in this time.

Rip up the basil and add it to the courgettes, then stir in the mascarpone and some black pepper (don't add any extra salt at this stage as the pecorino is very salty).

Meanwhile, cook the rigatoni in a pot of boiling salted water for 3 minutes less than the packet suggests. Take out the rigatoni with a slotted spoon and add it to the cooked courgettes. Add 2 ladlefuls of the pasta water, then half the grated pecorino, and stir well.

Cook over a low heat for a further 3 minutes, stirring or tossing the pan occasionally. Check the seasoning and serve in warm pasta bowls with the remaining pecorino sprinkled on top.

Zucchini, red pepper and tomato pizzette

Makes 8 small pizzas

For the pizza dough
1kg (2lb 3oz) tipo 00 flour,
   plus extra for dusting
5g (⅛oz) dried yeast
1 tsp sugar
2 tbsp olive oil
600ml (20fl oz) lukewarm
   water
20g (¾oz) salt
100g (3½oz) fine
   semolina flour

For the topping
6 tbsp extra-virgin olive oil
2 small red onions,
   finely sliced
1 garlic clove, finely sliced
1 tsp thyme leaves
   (not lemon thyme)
2 red (bell) peppers,
   deseeded and finely sliced
3 medium courgettes, sliced
   into 5mm (¼in) rounds
600ml (20fl oz) tomato passata
   (strained tomatoes), poured
   into a bowl
60g (2¼oz) miniature capers
   in vinegar, drained, or in
   salt, rinsed
20 taggiasche or niçoise
   olives, pitted and roughly
   chopped
2 tbsp marjoram leaves,
   finely chopped
250g (9oz) ricotta
sea salt and freshly ground
   black pepper

A pizzetta is a small pizza that is perfect as a snack and fun to make with a few people. If you have a pizza oven, then this is a must-try recipe; if you don't, a pizza stone that fits in your oven is a good idea. Otherwise, putting the oven on a high temperature with top and bottom elements on will work well, as long as your roasting tray is very clean and hot, so the pizzette don't stick.

Pizzette are more forgiving than a full size pizza – you don't have to stretch the dough so much and they can be cooked in batches of three at a time. I precook the peppers, onions and courgettes for maximum flavour, which also makes the pizzette a lot easier to finish off in the oven.

Place the tipo 00 flour in the bowl of a stand mixer with the dough hook attachment. In a jug (pitcher), combine the yeast, sugar, olive oil and water, then give it a good stir so the yeast dissolves. Turn the machine on a very low setting and start slowly pouring the yeasted water into the flour. Make sure the water gets absorbed after each pour and repeat this until all the water has been used. Keep the machine kneading the dough for a further 15 minutes until it becomes really smooth. Add the salt and keep kneading until all the salt has been absorbed.

Take the dough out and knead with your hands until you have a large, smooth ball (you may need a little more flour to help you knead). Place in an oiled bowl, cover with a damp tea (dish) towel, put in a warm place and leave to rise for 3 hours (yes, 3 hours – the dough will taste much better for it).

Pizza always cooks better if you cook it on a pizza stone in your oven, or better still a pizza oven in your garden (see intro). With a pizza stone or clean baking sheet already inside, preheat the oven to the highest it will go 1 hour before you start assembling the pizzetta.

Divide the risen dough into 8 pieces. Shape each piece into a ball, cover with a tea towel and leave to rise at room temperature for a further 30 minutes.

Meanwhile, make the topping. Add the olive oil to a hot, large non-stick frying pan, then add the onions, garlic, thyme, red peppers, courgettes and a generous pinch of salt. Cook over a medium heat for 15 minutes, stirring from time to time, until all the vegetables have become softer and are mixed together. Take off the heat and leave to cool.

Continued overleaf

Zucchini, red pepper and tomato pizzette
continued

Shape each dough ball into a small circle. The best way to do this is by hand, half hanging the dough over the edge of a work surface so that gravity helps to pull the dough while you are shaping it in a circular manner. This does take a bit of time and skill but is definitely worth mastering, as the result will be a lovely, light, crispy pizza. An easier method is to use a rolling pin – make an oval pizza by rolling lengthways until you've stretched out the dough. This will result in a crisp base with little to no raised crust (by using a rolling pin, you are removing the air from the dough), but the end result will still be tasty. Throughout shaping, use the semolina flour for dusting, to prevent the dough from sticking.

Once you have shaped your little pizzas, dollop a generous tablespoon of the passata onto each, using the spoon to spread the passata to the outer edges. Divide the cooked courgette mixture evenly between the pizzas, then scatter over the capers, olives and marjoram. Using a teaspoon, place small dollops of ricotta all over each pizza.

Preferably using a pizza slice, slide each pizza onto the hot pizza stone or baking sheet, leaving plenty of room between each. There may only be enough room to cook two at a time, which is fine, as it is important to make sure the pizzas cook well and evenly. Cook until the dough is cooked through and browning in places. Serve immediately, straight out of the oven and sprinkled with black pepper, while you cook the rest.

Zucchini and ricotta crespelle

Makes 8 medium pancakes

3 tbsp extra-virgin olive oil
2 medium onions, finely sliced
3 medium courgettes
 (zucchini), sliced into 1cm
 (½in) rounds
6 basil leaves
250g (9oz) ricotta
2 tbsp sunflower oil
sea salt and freshly ground
 black pepper

For the béchamel
500ml (17fl oz) whole milk
1 bay leaf
60g (2¼oz) butter
60g (2¼oz) plain
 (all-purpose) flour
150g (5½oz) parmesan,
 finely grated, plus extra
 to serve

For the pangrattato
2 slices of good-quality,
 dry bread
4 tbsp extra-virgin olive oil
1 tsp thyme leaves

For the pancake batter
4 eggs
50g (1¾oz) plain
 (all-purpose) flour
350ml (12fl oz) whole milk

These baked pancakes are perfect for lunch or a substantial snack served with drinks. They can also be made a day ahead, removing some of the stress of assembling the dish.

Pancakes are easy to make as long as you have a very good non-stick frying pan. If you don't have one, take your pan and place 500g (1lb 2oz) salt in it and place over a high heat for 5 minutes. When the pan seems really hot, take an old tea (dish) towel and, with your hand in an oven glove so you don't burn yourself, rub the salt into the pan using the tea towel. When you feel the pan is scrubbed clean by the salt, discard the baked salt. Add some sunflower oil to the pan and rub it in with kitchen paper, making sure the inside of the pan is completely covered in oil. The pan will now be non-stick.

Add the olive oil to a hot, large, non-stick frying pan, then add the onions and cook for 5 minutes. Add the courgettes and cook for a further 15 minutes; the courgettes should be soft and have a little colour on them. Add the basil leaves and season with salt and black pepper. Place the cooked courgettes and onions in a bowl and leave to cool. When cool, stir through the ricotta and season with salt and black pepper. Leave to one side.

Make the béchamel. Add the milk and bay leaf to a saucepan, bring to the boil, then take off the heat and set aside to infuse. Melt the butter in another saucepan set over a low–medium heat, then add the flour and cook for a couple of minutes, mixing with a wooden spoon. Next, slowly pour in the hot infused milk, beginning with a little at a time, stirring continuously to avoid any lumps. If there are any lumps, beat the béchamel with a balloon whisk; this will make the sauce smooth and silky. Once all the milk has been added, cook for 15 minutes, then remove the bay leaf, add the parmesan and season with salt and black pepper. Stir well, then remove from the heat and leave to one side.

For the pangrattato, whiz the bread in a food processor to fine crumbs. Add the olive oil to a hot saucepan, add the thyme, then the breadcrumbs and cook over a low heat, stirring all the time, so the breadcrumbs absorb the oil and start to turn a golden brown. Once evenly golden brown, tip them onto a piece of kitchen paper to absorb the excess oil, then sprinkle with some salt and leave to one side.

Continued overleaf

Zucchini and ricotta crespelle
continued

Now make the pancake batter. Whisk the eggs with the flour and a pinch of salt. Slowly add the milk and whisk until the batter has a smooth texture. Cover with cling film (plastic wrap) and rest in the fridge for 20 minutes.

Add the sunflower oil to a hot non-stick frying pan, and move it around the pan so all sides are covered, then pour out the excess oil. Fill a ladle with the pancake mixture and pour it into the middle of the pan. Lift and tilt the pan so the mixture fills the flat part of the frying pan, forming a round pancake. Cook for 2 minutes over a medium heat, then flip the pancake over. The best way to do this is to turn up the heat and then, using a spiralling motion with the pan, flip it over onto the other side. Cook for another couple of minutes, then remove the pancake from the pan and place on a chopping board. Repeat until you have cooked all the mixture. This should be enough for 8 pancakes.

To put the crespelle together, place each pancake on a chopping board and divide the courgette mixture evenly between each, so it is roughly in a line in the middle of the pancake. Lift one side of the pancake up and over the filling and secure it tightly, then roll forwards to make a long cylinder. Place the 8 rolled pancakes snugly in an oiled baking dish. Pour over the béchamel to cover the pancakes. At this stage, you can cover and refrigerate the dish until the next day (if desired).

Preheat the oven to 180°C/160°C fan/350°F/Gas 4.

Bake the crespelle for 20 minutes until bubbling, then cover the top with the pangrattato. Place the cooked dish in the middle of the table and serve on warm plates with a little extra parmesan grated over the top.

Penne with cime di zucca and datterini tomatoes

Serves 6

1 head and stem of a
  courgette (zucchini) or
  squash plant, trimmed of
  tough outer leaves
9 tbsp extra-virgin olive oil
2 garlic cloves, finely sliced
1 tbsp chopped oregano
1 red chilli, deseeded and
  finely chopped
200g (7oz) datterini tomatoes,
  quartered
600ml (20fl oz) tomato passata
  (strained tomatoes)
500g (1lb 2oz) dried
  penne rigate
sea salt and freshly ground
  black pepper
freshly grated parmesan,
  to serve

Italian food is frugal, and this recipe proves it. Cime di zucca is basically the courgette or squash plant. It can be large and may look unappealing, but cooked it has the most wonderful flavour. You need to cut off all the tough outer leaves and trim off any part you don't like the look of. Combined with a rich tomato sauce, this becomes a very tasty dish and a perfect way to use up something you would not normally cook.

Wash the head of the courgette plant really well in cold water. Cut into 8 pieces and place in a large pan of boiling water with 1 teaspoon of salt. Cook over a medium heat for 25 minutes, then test by sliding a sharp knife through the centre of a piece of courgette plant; if the knife goes through without any resistance, it is cooked. Drain into a colander and leave to cool. When cool, chop into a rough pulp.

Add 3 tablespoons of the olive oil to a hot, very large frying pan, then add half the garlic and the chopped oregano and chilli. Cook for 1 minute, then add the tomatoes. Cook over a low heat for 5 minutes, then add the passata and cook for 10 minutes. Pour the sauce into a bowl and leave to one side.

Wash the frying pan and place it back over the heat with another 3 tablespoons of the olive oil and the remaining garlic. Cook for 30 seconds, then add the chopped cooled courgette plant and cook over a medium heat for 15 minutes, until the moisture from the courgette plant has evaporated and it is starting to slightly colour. Season with salt and black pepper, add the tomato sauce and cook over a low heat for 15 minutes.

Meanwhile, cook the penne in a pot of boiling salted water for 3 minutes less than the packet suggests. Take the pasta out of the water with a slotted spoon and add it directly to the courgette plant and tomato sauce in the frying pan, keeping the pasta water on the stove. Add a ladleful of the pasta water and start stirring or tossing the pasta and the sauce. Cook and toss for 3 minutes, then add the remaining 3 tablespoons of olive oil.

Check the seasoning and serve immediately with a sprinkling of parmesan and black pepper on top.

Risotto stuffed zucchini

Serves 4

4 large courgettes (zucchini)
3 tbsp extra-virgin olive oil
1 medium onion, finely
  chopped
2 celery stalks, finely chopped
150g (5¹⁄₂oz) Carnaroli
  risotto rice
100ml (3¹⁄₂fl oz) dry white wine
300ml (10fl oz) tomato passata
  (strained tomatoes)
600ml (20fl oz) hot vegetable
  stock (see page 19 for
  homemade)
4 basil leaves
75g (2¹⁄₂oz) unsalted butter
75g (2¹⁄₂oz) parmesan, grated
sea salt and freshly ground
  black pepper

For the topping
100g (3¹⁄₂oz) breadcrumbs
1 tsp thyme leaves
2 tbsp extra-virgin olive oil,
  plus extra to finish
1 garlic clove, crushed to
  a paste with a little sea salt
75g (2¹⁄₂oz) parmesan, grated,
  plus extra to finish

This recipe is a great way to use up oversized courgettes that may be a little past their best, or just a bit spongy. My mother used to make a delicious stuffed marrow, which is the inspiration for this dish. This is essentially a risotto made from the insides of the courgettes and then put back in and baked. The breadcrumbs add lots of texture and flavour and also soak up some of the roasting juices.

Cut the tops and ends off the courgettes and carefully cut in half lengthways. Place the courgette halves on a flat tray and sprinkle 1 teaspoon of salt over the cut sides. Leave for 20 minutes so that they release some of their water, then pat dry with some kitchen paper. Place the courgettes flat-side up and, using a small teaspoon, scoop out the centre seed channel of each half, leaving a boat shape and reserving the scooped-out pulp.

Add the olive oil to a hot, straight-sided saucepan, then add the onion, celery and rice. Cook, stirring for 3 minutes, so the rice absorbs the olive oil and goes translucent. Add the wine and cook until it is absorbed, then add the passata and scooped-out courgette pulp. Start adding the hot stock, a ladleful at a time, so the rice is always just covered; keep doing this for 15 minutes over a medium heat. Season with salt and black pepper, then stir through the basil, butter and parmesan. Place the cooked rice on a flat tray so it cools down quickly. Once the rice has cooled, spoon the mixture generously into the scooped-out courgette halves.

Place the courgette halves on a roasting tray and preheat the oven to 160°C/140°C fan/320°F/Gas 3.

Add the topping ingredients to a bowl and mix thoroughly until combined, then sprinkle over the filled courgette halves, so the rice is covered.

Bake in the oven for 25 minutes, until the courgettes are cooked all the way through. Serve immediately sprinkled with a little extra parmesan and olive oil.

Cheesy tagliarini with grated zucchini and pangrattato

**Serves 2 as a main course
or 4 as a starter**

3 medium courgettes
(zucchini)
3 tbsp extra-virgin olive oil
1 garlic clove, finely sliced
1 tbsp chopped flat-leaf
parsley
150g (5½oz) mascarpone
150g (5½oz) parmesan, grated
250g (9oz) fresh tagliarini
pasta
sea salt and freshly ground
black pepper

For the pangrattato
2 slices of good-quality,
dry bread
4 tbsp extra-virgin olive oil
1 tsp thyme leaves

**Grated courgette works really nicely in this recipe, and it
cooks very quickly, so this is a very speedy plate of pasta.
The pangrattato brings lots of flavour and crunch – a nice
addition to any creamy pasta. Medium-sized courgettes work
best for this recipe as they tend to be less watery than large
ones. If you only have large ones, add a pinch of salt to the
grated courgettes and leave them in a bowl for 5 minutes.
Take a tea (dish) towel and place the salted courgettes in
the middle, then give them a good squeeze to extract the
excess water.**

Cut both ends off each courgette and grate on the coarse side
of a box grater.

Add the olive oil to a large non-stick frying pan over a medium
heat, then add the garlic and cook for 30 seconds. Add the
grated courgettes and a good pinch of salt, then cook for
15 minutes, stirring occasionally so the courgettes get a bit
of colour. Add the parsley, mascarpone and parmesan, and stir
so all the ingredients are well mixed and everything in the pan
is starting to resemble a thick sauce. Take off the heat and leave
to one side.

For the pangrattato, whiz the bread in a food processor to fine
crumbs. Add the olive oil to a hot saucepan, add the thyme,
then the breadcrumbs and cook over a low heat, stirring all the
time, so the breadcrumbs absorb the oil and start to go a golden
brown. Once evenly golden brown, tip them onto a piece of
kitchen paper to absorb the excess oil, sprinkle with some
salt and leave to one side.

Place the courgette mixture back over a low heat. Cook the
tagliarini in a large pot of boiling salted water for 2 minutes,
then remove with a pair of tongs and add to the courgette
sauce, along with 1 ladleful of the pasta water. Stir or toss and,
if needed, add another ladleful of pasta water, making sure the
sauce is creamy and coats the strands of pasta.

Serve in warm bowls with a generous amount of pangrattato
scattered over each portion, and some black pepper on top.

ASPARAGUS

Green asparagus salad with roasted salted almonds

Serves 4 as a side

500g (1lb 2oz) asparagus
  spears, tough ends removed
250g (9oz) fine green beans,
  topped and tailed
200g (7oz) podded fresh peas
  or frozen petits pois
400g (14oz) baby leaf spinach
10 mint leaves
sea salt and freshly ground
  black pepper

For the dressing
zest and juice of 1 orange
2 tbsp honey
1 tbsp white balsamic vinegar
4 tbsp extra-virgin olive oil

For the roasted, salted almonds
100g (3½oz) whole blanched
  almonds
1 tsp extra-virgin olive oil
1 tsp water
good pinch of salt

When grilling asparagus it is important to blanch the spears first, otherwise they become stringy and a bit dry. This is a simple salad and perfect for eating al fresco. The roasted almond, orange and honey combination is very tasty. I have used white balsamic here but white wine vinegar works just as well.

Preheat the oven to 180°C/160°C fan/350°F/Gas 4.

First make the dressing. Add the orange zest and juice, honey and vinegar to a medium bowl, mix together with a whisk, then slowly add all the olive oil so the dressing is emulsified. Season with salt and black pepper and leave to one side.

Cook the asparagus in a pan of boiling salted water for 2 minutes. Take out with a slotted spoon and leave the asparagus to drain and cool down; do not refresh in cold water or it will make the asparagus waterlogged and dilute its natural flavour.

Add the green beans to the boiling water you used for the asparagus and cook for about 5 minutes, then remove from the water and leave to drain and cool down. Again, do not refresh in cold water. Blanch the peas in the same water for 1 minute, then drain and leave to cool down.

Heat a griddle pan or heavy frying pan until very hot. Place the asparagus spears on the griddle pan, then after 2 minutes turn them and cook for another 2 minutes; they should have a nice light charring on all sides. Place on a chopping board and cut each stem in half lengthways.

Put the almonds in a bowl with the olive oil and water, and a good pinch of salt. Mix, then spread out on a baking sheet and cook in the oven for 10 minutes or until a light golden brown. Remove and tip onto kitchen paper to absorb any excess oil. Leave to cool.

Take a large serving bowl or deep plate and place the spinach leaves on the bottom. Scatter over the green beans, asparagus, peas and mint leaves, and finish off with the roasted almonds scattered on top. Serve at the table with the dressing poured over evenly, just as you are ready to eat.

Asparagus fritto with saffron aioli

Serves 4 as a starter

16 asparagus spears
  (all roughly the same size),
  tough ends removed
500ml (17fl oz) sunflower oil
60g (2¼oz) tipo 00 flour
sea salt

For the saffron aioli
3 egg yolks
1 garlic clove, crushed to
  a paste with a little sea salt
1 tsp Dijon mustard
juice of 1 lemon
1g (pinch) saffron threads,
  soaked in 3 tbsp hot water
250ml (9fl oz) light extra-virgin
  olive oil

For the batter
300g (10½oz) tipo 00 flour
4 tbsp extra-virgin olive oil
250ml (9fl oz) warm water
1 egg white, beaten

Asparagus is made for deep-frying, the perfect size for dipping into a batter and cooking until crispy. Make sure they are dry before dipping them in the batter, or the batter will not stick. Saffron is a strong taste but I think it goes nicely with the concentrated asparagus flavour. If you don't have any saffron, aioli on its own works well. Serve these little beauties hot with a sprinkle of sea salt and a paper napkin.

Make the saffron aioli. In a ceramic or plastic bowl (do not use a metal bowl as it will make the aioli taste metallic) combine the egg yolks, crushed garlic in salt, mustard, lemon juice and saffron water. Using a whisk or stick blender, mix until smooth. Slowly add the olive oil, whisking all the time, until it has all been used and the mixture is thick and very yellow. Place to one side.

Add the asparagus spears to a large pan of boiling salted water and cook for 2 minutes. Drain, place on a flat tray and pop in the fridge to cool down; do not run them under cold water as this will make them waterlogged. When the asparagus has cooled, pat dry with some kitchen paper and leave to one side.

To make the batter, put the flour into a large bowl, make a well in the middle and pour in the olive oil. Using a whisk, mix the oil and flour together and slowly add the warm water to achieve the consistency of double (heavy) cream. Leave for 20 minutes in the fridge. Take out and carefully fold in the beaten egg white. Place back in the fridge until ready to use.

Heat the sunflower oil in a large, deep frying pan or deep-fat fryer until it reads 170°C/325°F on a cooking thermometer or a drop of batter sizzles and browns in 10 seconds.

Place the tipo 00 flour on a flat tray and sprinkle over a little salt. Roll the asparagus one at a time in the flour, so all the spears are covered in a light dusting of flour; this will help the batter stick. One by one, dip each floured spear into the batter, then knock off any excess batter and gently drop into the hot sunflower oil (fry in batches so you don't overcrowd the pan). Once the asparagus has a light golden colour, remove from the oil with a slotted spoon and place on a wire rack with a tray underneath to collect any excess oil (if you drain them on kitchen paper they tend to go soggy). The asparagus should have enough salt but add more if you like them a bit salty.

Serve hot on a platter along with the saffron aioli in a nice bowl for dipping.

Grilled polenta with warm asparagus and tomato salad

Serves 4 as a starter

400g (14oz) asparagus
  spears, tough ends removed
3 tbsp water
1 tsp thyme leaves
2 tbsp extra-virgin olive oil,
  plus extra to finish
1 garlic clove, finely sliced
150g (5½oz) datterini
  tomatoes, halved
50g (1¾oz) pitted taggiasche
  or niçoise olives
25g (1oz) miniature capers
  in vinegar, drained
1 tbsp chopped flat-leaf
  parsley
150g (5½oz) parmesan
  shavings
sea salt

For the polenta
400ml (14fl oz) water
100g (3½oz) Bramata polenta
  (coarse cornmeal)

Cooking asparagus this way gives you maximum flavour because it steams in its own moisture. Datterini tomatoes add a lovely sweetness and, combined with the salty olives, parmesan shavings and grilled polenta, make a delicious starter. Thick-ish asparagus is best here, as it will withstand the high temperature it is cooked at. I love grilled polenta and love asparagus, and this recipe is a wonderful way to eat them both.

To make the set polenta, heat the water in a large saucepan, add a pinch of salt and, when simmering, add the polenta in a steady stream, using a balloon whisk to stir it in; it's important you add it gradually, so the polenta can be dispersed evenly and will therefore cook evenly. Once you have added all the polenta, turn down the heat and cook gently for 30 minutes, until the polenta is starting to come away from the edges of the pan. Pour into a straight-sided ceramic dish so the polenta is 2cm (¾in) thick. Leave to cool and set firm.

Place the asparagus spears in a hot non-stick frying pan with the water, thyme, olive oil, garlic and a pinch of salt. Put the lid on the pan and cook over a medium heat for 4 minutes, moving the pan occasionally so the asparagus cooks evenly. Add the tomatoes, olives, capers and parsley, place the lid back on and cook for a further 3 minutes. Take off the lid, remove from the heat and keep warm on the side.

Cut the set polenta into 4 slices, each 5cm (2in) wide. Heat a griddle pan until very hot, then place the polenta slices on the griddle pan. Leave for 4 minutes, without touching them. It is important that the polenta forms a crust, which will make it easier to turn it over and also enhance the flavour. Turn over each slice carefully and cook until crispy on the other side. Place the polenta on plates and divide the warm asparagus salad between them. Cover with parmesan shavings and a drizzle of olive oil.

Asparagus, leek and potato soup with pesto

Serves 4

300g (10½oz) asparagus
spears, tough stems
removed, sliced into 1cm
(½in) pieces
75g (2½oz) butter
1 tsp thyme leaves
2 medium leeks, cut into
2cm (¾in) pieces
500g (1lb 2oz) Désirée or
Cyprus potatoes, peeled and
cut into 2cm (¾in) pieces
100ml (3½fl oz) double
(heavy) cream
sea salt and freshly ground
black pepper

For the pesto
½ garlic clove
pinch of sea salt
100g (3½oz) basil leaves
75g (2½oz) pine nuts
(untoasted)
75g (2½oz) parmesan,
finely grated
2 tbsp water
150ml (5fl oz) extra-virgin
olive oil, plus extra to finish

Asparagus and pesto add something really special to this classic combination. The soup works better by puréeing only half of it, as the texture of the asparagus gives the soup another dimension; pesto makes it fresher, too. This can be served in little cups for some sustenance at a stand-up drinks party, or just as a good old bowl of creamy soup.

To make the pesto, in a pestle and mortar, crush the half garlic clove with the salt to a fine paste. Add the basil and crush until the leaves are pulped, then add the pine nuts, crush to a paste, then add the parmesan, followed by the water. Mix so everything is emulsified, then slowly stir in the olive oil. Keep to one side.

In a large, heavy-based saucepan filled halfway with salted boiling water (about 2 litres/68fl oz) add the asparagus and cook for 2 minutes, then drain into a colander, reserving the cooking water in a jug (pitcher).

Give the saucepan a rinse and wipe with some kitchen paper. Place the pan back over a medium heat and add the butter and thyme, so the butter melts. Add the leeks, potatoes and a good pinch of salt. Cook for 15 minutes, stirring occasionally. Add 1 litre (34fl oz) of the asparagus cooking water and cook for 10 minutes. Check the potatoes are soft by putting a knife through them; if there is no resistance, they are cooked.

Using a stick blender or food processor, purée half the soup and place back in the pan. Add the cream and bring back to a simmer. If you feel the soup is too thick, add another 100ml (3½fl oz) of the asparagus water. Add the blanched asparagus and a generous spoonful of pesto to the soup. Check the seasoning, serve in warm bowls, and finish with another spoonful of pesto in each and a drizzle of extra-virgin olive oil.

Asparagus tagliatelle with wild garlic cream

Serves 4 as a starter

200ml (7fl oz) double
(heavy) cream
100g (3½oz) wild garlic,
washed and roughly
chopped into 2cm
(¾in) pieces
300g (10½oz) asparagus
spears, tough ends removed,
sliced at an angle
250g (9oz) dried tagliatelle
100g (3½oz) pecorino, grated
sea salt and freshly ground
black pepper

I remember the scent of wild garlic as a kid, and never really liked it. An easy way to convince me to eat it would be this pasta – cooked with cream it is very tasty. That, and my foraging friend Martine's wild garlic pesto, which I very much enjoy when I visit her in Camargue in the south of France. English asparagus and wild garlic cross over in season, so this is a dish to cook in early spring to welcome in more light-filled days.

Add the cream to a hot, large, non-stick frying pan and bring to a simmer. Add the wild garlic and cook gently for 5 minutes so the leaves are wilted and soft.

Add the asparagus pieces to a large pan of boiling salted water and cook for 3 minutes. Remove with a slotted spoon, keeping the water, and add the asparagus to the wild garlic and cream.

Add the tagliatelle to the asparagus cooking water, bring the water back to the boil and cook until the pasta has a nice bite still. Remove the pasta from the cooking water with a pair of tongs, again keeping the water, and add the tagliatelle to the frying pan with the asparagus, cream and wild garlic.

Add a ladleful of the pasta water to the pan and turn up the heat. Stir or toss the pasta so it starts to emulsify, add half the grated pecorino and keep stirring or tossing gently so as not to break the tagliatelle. Check the seasoning and add some freshly ground black pepper.

Serve in warm pasta bowls with the remaining pecorino sprinkled on top.

Paccheri with asparagus, porcini and butter

Serves 4 as a starter

25g (1oz) dried porcini
400ml (14fl oz) boiling water
100g (3½oz) butter
1 tsp thyme leaves
1 garlic clove, finely sliced
300g (10½oz) asparagus
  spears, tough ends removed,
  sliced at an angle
300g (10½oz) dried
  paccheri pasta
150g (5½oz) parmesan, grated
sea salt and freshly ground
  black pepper

Paccheri pasta is officially my favourite dried pasta. Well, it is while I am writing this... The texture is amazing – when cooked, the round tubes become like a sponge and collect the sauce, almost like a vacuum, so every paccheri tube has the pleasurable surprise of a saucy inside. I love the combination of porcini mushroom and asparagus, but if you are really lucky and have managed to get hold of some fresh morels, then this is the recipe to use them in.

Add the dried porcini to a medium bowl, pour over the boiling water to cover and leave to soak for 15 minutes. Take out the porcini and place on a chopping board. Using a small, sharp knife, scrape off any visible grit (this will be on the base of the mushroom). Give the cleaned porcini a wash, pat dry, then chop finely. Strain the soaking juice through a fine piece of kitchen paper, or better still a paper coffee filter, and keep to one side.

Add the butter, thyme and garlic to a hot, large non-stick frying pan, cook for 1 minute, then add the chopped porcini and the reserved soaking liquid. Turn down the heat to low and cook until the liquid has reduced by half.

Add the asparagus to a large pan of boiling salted water and cook for 3 minutes. Remove from the pan with a slotted spoon, leaving the water in the pan, and add to the porcini mixture. Leave to one side while you cook the paccheri.

Cook the paccheri, in the boiling water you cooked the asparagus in, for 2 minutes less than the packet suggests. Remove the paccheri from the water with a slotted spoon and transfer to the asparagus and porcini pan. Add a ladleful of the pasta cooking water, place the pan over a high heat and reduce the liquid for about 3 minutes.

Add half the parmesan and stir the pasta so the parmesan mixes with the sauce, adding another ladleful of pasta water if there is not enough liquid. Wiggle the pan so all the sauce is coating the pasta. Check the seasoning and serve in warm bowls with some ground black pepper and the remaining grated parmesan on top.

Asparagus and potato gnocchi with ricotta and sage

Serves 4 as a starter

1kg (2lb 3oz) Désirée (or
  other red) potatoes, similar
  size, washed with skins on
2 eggs, beaten
200g (7oz) tipo 00 flour, plus
  extra for dusting
300g (10½oz) asparagus
  spears, tough stems
  removed, sliced at an angle
  into 2cm (¾in) pieces
150g (5½oz) unsalted butter
12 sage leaves
1 garlic clove, finely sliced
150g (5½oz) parmesan,
  finely grated
200g (7oz) ricotta, seasoned
  with sea salt, freshly ground
  black pepper and olive oil
sea salt and freshly ground
  black pepper

Potato gnocchi is not complicated to make, and the general rule is, the less flour used the lighter the gnocchi. It is best eaten on the day it is made, and in Rome they always eat it on a Thursday. You will see signs outside trattorias saying what the week's specialities are, and Thursday is always gnocchi day. It tastes the same any day of the week but it just goes to show it has to be eaten fresh.

The brown butter, asparagus and fresh ricotta taste delicious with the soft, chewy potato gnocchi and crispy sage. Thank god it's Thursday!

Add the potatoes to a large saucepan, fill the pan with cold water and add 1 teaspoon of salt. Bring to the boil, then turn down the heat and cook gently for 30 minutes. Check by pushing a skewer through; if there is no resistance, they are cooked. Drain into a colander.

When the potatoes are a bit cooler, but still warm, cut them in half and, using a tablespoon, scoop out the insides. Push the flesh through a potato ricer or mouli, into a bowl. Add the eggs, then fold in the flour. Place the mixture on a floured work surface and lightly knead with your hands until all the ingredients have combined well.

Divide into 4 equal pieces and roll each into a long sausage, using the palms of each hand. Cut each long sausage into 3cm (1¼in) pieces and dust a little flour on top. Take each piece and roll it over the back of an upturned folk (see overleaf), then place carefully in a single layer on a floured tray. Place the tray in the fridge but do not cover with cling film (plastic wrap) as the gnocchi will become soggy. If you want to cover them to cook the next day, cover with baking paper and secure with large elastic bands.

Heat a large pan of boiling salted water, add the asparagus and cook for 3 minutes, then remove and keep to one side, keeping the water to cook the gnocchi in later.

Add half the butter to a hot, large, non-stick frying pan and cook over a medium heat until the butter starts to foam, then add the sage and cook until the leaves go crispy and the butter slightly brown. Take out the crispy sage with a slotted spoon and transfer the browned butter to a bowl.

Add the remaining butter to the hot frying pan you just cooked the sage in, over a low heat, and add the garlic and cooked asparagus.

Bring the asparagus cooking water back to the boil, then add the gnocchi a few at a time. When all the gnocchi are in the water and are starting to rise, take them out with a slotted spoon and place them in the frying pan with the asparagus, adding a ladleful or two of the cooking water. Add half the parmesan, wiggle the pan and stir the gnocchi gently so they don't break.

Once the sauce has emulsified and the gnocchi are coated, serve in warm pasta bowls with the seasoned ricotta, fried sage and reserved browned butter on top of each. Finish with the remaining parmesan and plenty of black pepper.

Pictured overleaf

Morel and asparagus risotto with roasted garlic cream

Serves 4 as a starter

1 whole garlic bulb
4 tbsp extra-virgin olive oil
1 thyme sprig
100ml (3½fl oz) milk
100ml (3½fl oz) double
  (heavy) cream
250g (9oz) asparagus spears,
  tough stems removed
20g (¾oz) dried morel
  mushrooms or 100g
  (3½oz) fresh
2 tbsp finely chopped celery
1 medium white onion,
  finely chopped
200g (7oz) Carnaroli
  risotto rice
100ml (3½fl oz) dry white wine
2 litres (68fl oz) hot vegetable
  stock (see page 19 for
  homemade)
100g (3½oz) butter
100g (3½oz) parmesan,
  grated, plus extra to serve
sea salt and freshly ground
  black pepper

Fresh wild morel mushrooms are the most expensive mushrooms on the planet and are also only available in spring – they like a sudden change in temperature from very cold to warmer weather. Fortunately, they seem to cultivate reasonably well in places like Turkey and China, which now makes them cheaper and easier to get hold of. I have used dried cultivated ones in this recipe and the taste is excellent. If you can't get hold of dried morels, you can substitute them with dried porcini mushrooms – porcini haven't been successfully cultivated so are always wild and therefore full of flavour.

If you have a foraging friend or are a forager yourself, using fresh wild morels is very special, and this is the perfect dish to celebrate them.

Preheat the oven to 180°C/160°C fan/350°F/Gas 4.

Soak the garlic bulb in warm water for 10 minutes. Take a sheet of foil and pour 1 tablespoon of the olive oil into the middle, then add the wet garlic bulb, the thyme sprig, and some salt and black pepper. Wrap the foil around the garlic bulb, place on a baking tray and cook in the oven for 35 minutes. Take out and leave to cool. When cool, unwrap the foil and squeeze out the roasted cloves; they should be golden brown and soft. Place the roasted garlic in a small saucepan with the milk and cream and cook gently until reduced by half. Using a stick blender or whisk, mash the garlic and cream so it is smooth and thick. Check the seasoning.

Cook the asparagus for 3 minutes in a pan of boiling salted water. Drain into a colander and leave to cool. When the asparagus has cooled down, cut into 1cm (½in) pieces and leave to one side.

Soak the dried morels (unless using fresh) in just-boiled water for 10 minutes. Strain the liquid through some kitchen paper or a paper coffee filter, catching the liquid below, and inspect the morels to make sure there is no grit on them. Cut them in half lengthways. Heat 1 tablespoon of the oil in a saucepan and fry the morels until soft, then add the strained soaking liquid and cook gently until it has reduced and is syrupy. If you are lucky to have fresh morels, skip the soaking, clean them very carefully and fry them the same way (there is no need to add extra liquid as the fresh morels will release moisture). Season and keep to one side.

Continued overleaf

Morel and asparagus risotto with roasted garlic cream
continued

Add the remaining 2 tablespoons of olive oil to a hot, large, straight-sided saucepan, then add the celery and onion. Cook over a medium heat for 3 minutes then add the rice and cook for a further 3 minutes so the rice absorbs the oil and goes translucent. Add the wine and cook until it is absorbed, then start adding the stock, a ladleful at a time, so the rice is always just covered. Keep doing this for 10 minutes over a medium heat so the rice is bubbling away. Add the cooked morels and continue adding stock for a further 5 minutes. Add the cooked asparagus pieces and a little more stock and cook for a further 3 minutes, stirring all the time. Add the butter and parmesan and, when they have melted into the risotto, take off the heat. Mix the risotto vigorously, check the seasoning, then place a lid on top and leave on the side for 2 minutes.

Take the lid off the risotto and stir thoroughly so it is creamy. Check the seasoning again. Serve in warm bowls with a spoonful of the roasted garlic cream in the middle of each portion, and a little extra parmesan and some black pepper on top.

Ricotta and asparagus ravioli with walnut sauce

Serves 4

For the pasta dough
350g (12oz) tipo 00 flour
25g (1oz) fine semolina flour,
  plus 50g (1¾oz) for dusting
2 whole eggs, plus 4 egg
  yolks, beaten together
2 tbsp water

For the filling
500g (1lb 2oz) asparagus
  spears, tough ends removed
1 tbsp extra-virgin olive oil
1 tbsp thyme leaves
250g (9oz) ricotta
60g (2¼oz) breadcrumbs
75g (2½oz) parmesan, grated
1 egg
sea salt and freshly ground
  black pepper

For the walnut sauce
½ garlic clove
pinch of sea salt
120g (4oz) shelled walnuts
25g (1oz) parmesan, plus
  extra to serve
25g (1oz) breadcrumbs
100ml (3½fl oz) milk
50ml (1¾fl oz) extra-virgin
  olive oil

**Ravioli take time and planning, but once they are made
the only thing left to do is cook them, so these are great for
a dinner party, as the prep is done before your guests arrive.
Make sure you chop the roasted asparagus finely, as you
don't want any bits poking through the pasta. Walnut sauce
is lovely with the asparagus ravioli and tastes even better
with freshly cracked walnuts, but they are harder to find
than shelled walnuts; just make sure the packet ones are
from a fresh packet.**

**You can make the ravioli the day before you serve it, but
don't cover them with cling film (plastic wrap) as this will
make them go soggy.**

Make the pasta dough. Add both flours to a large bowl, mix
together, then add the beaten eggs and water. Mix together
with a fork then, when combined, use your hands to start forming
a dough. Once the dough is smooth, wrap it in cling film (plastic
wrap) and place in the fridge for 20 minutes.

Preheat the oven to 180°C/160°C fan/350°F/Gas 4.

Cook the asparagus spears in a pan of boiling salted water
for 3 minutes. Drain and toss in a large bowl with the olive oil
and thyme, and some salt and black pepper to taste. Place the
asparagus on a roasting tray and cook for 10 minutes in the
hot oven, then remove and leave to cool down. Finely chop the
asparagus and mix with the ricotta, breadcrumbs, parmesan
and egg. Check the seasoning and put to one side.

To make the walnut sauce, in a pestle and mortar, crush the
garlic with the salt, add the walnuts and crush to a paste, then
add the parmesan, breadcrumbs and milk. Stir thoroughly while
slowly adding the olive oil until the sauce is emulsified.

Divide the pasta dough into 4 equal pieces. Take one of the
pieces and, using a rolling pin, roll until the dough is thin enough
to go through the rollers on your pasta machine. Place one
end in the machine on the widest setting and roll it through the
machine. Fold the pasta in half and roll again. Repeat 4 times
for each quarter of pasta. This process makes the pasta more
elastic so it will be much more durable and won't break. Roll
each quarter of pasta into long sheets – when you can see the
silhouette of your hand behind the pasta, it is thin enough.

Continued overleaf

Ricotta and asparagus ravioli with walnut sauce
continued

Place one sheet on the work surface, dusted with semolina flour to stop the pasta from sticking. Place a teaspoonful of the roasted asparagus filling on the pasta sheet and then leave a 2-fingerwidth space before adding another teaspoonful. Continue until you reach the end of the pasta sheet. Using a pastry brush, brush water in between the filling and on the edge of the pasta. Carefully fold over the lengths of pasta sheet, encasing the filling. Using your fingertips, push down so you create little individual parcels. Cup your hand around the filling and push down gently on the ravioli to remove any unwanted air pockets. Take a pasta cutter and cut out the ravioli into individual pieces. Place on a tray with a good dusting of semolina flour on it so the pasta doesn't stick to the tray. Repeat this process until you have used all the dough and filling.

To cook the ravioli, add them to a large pan of boiling salted water and cook for 3 minutes. Remove with a slotted spoon and add to a warm, large, non-stick frying pan with half the walnut sauce and a ladleful of the pasta cooking water. Move the pan around so the starch from the pasta thickens the sauce. Serve in hot pasta bowls with the remaining sauce drizzled on top of the ravioli and extra parmesan and black pepper on top.

Mushroom, spinach and asparagus saccottini

Makes 24

2 tbsp extra-virgin olive oil
250g (9oz) chestnut (cremini)
  mushrooms, sliced
250g (9oz) asparagus spears,
  tough ends removed
400g (14oz) spinach
150g (5½oz) taleggio cheese,
  rind removed, finely chopped
150g (5½oz) mascarpone
100g (3½oz) unsalted butter
sea salt and freshly ground
  black pepper

For the pasta dough
350g (12oz) tipo 00 flour
25g (1oz) fine semolina flour,
  plus 50g (1¾oz) for dusting
2 whole eggs, plus 4 egg
  yolks, beaten together
2 tbsp water

Saccottini are one of the simpler and less-fiddly filled pastas to make. You can understand why they are also called 'beggar's purse' because of their bag-like shape. I have combined asparagus, spinach, taleggio and mushrooms for the filling, so when you eat these little pastas they are full of flavour. If you have never made stuffed fresh pasta before, then this is a great recipe to start with.

Make the pasta dough. Combine both flours in a large bowl, then add the beaten eggs and water. Mix together with a fork then, when combined, use your hands to start forming a dough. Once the dough is smooth, wrap it in cling film (plastic wrap) and place in the fridge for 20 minutes.

Add the olive oil to a hot, small frying pan, then add the mushrooms and cook for 10 minutes or until they are reduced, dark and slightly sticky. Season with salt and black pepper and leave to cool, then finely chop and keep to one side.

Cook the asparagus in a pan of boiling salted water for 3 minutes, then remove from the pan with a pair of tongs, keeping the water in the pan, and leave to cool down. Blanch the spinach in the boiling asparagus water for 1 minute after the water has come back to the boil, then drain into a colander. When the spinach has cooled, squeeze with a cloth so it is dry. Finely chop, then place in a bowl. Finely chop the asparagus and place in the bowl too. Add the cooked chopped mushrooms and the taleggio and mascarpone, and mix with a wooden spoon so the mixture is well combined. Season and keep to one side.

Divide the pasta into 4 equal pieces. Take one of the pieces and, on a work surface dusted with semolina flour, use a rolling pin to roll out the dough until thin enough to go through the rollers on your pasta machine. Place one end in the machine on the widest setting and roll it through the machine. Fold the pasta in half and roll again. Repeat 4 times for each quarter of pasta. This process makes the pasta more elastic so it will be much more durable and won't break. Roll each quarter of pasta into long sheets – when you can see the silhouette of your hand behind the pasta, it is thin enough. On a work surface dusted with semolina flour, cut out a 7cm (2¾in) square of pasta from one of the sheets, then use this as a template to cut all the pasta into equal squares. Place the cut-out squares in a single layer, with a damp tea (dish) towel on top.

Place a generous teaspoon of the filling mixture in the centre of each pasta square. Using a water sprayer or a wet pastry brush, wet the outside edges of the pasta. Bring 2 opposite corners together to meet in the middle, then do the same with the other 2 corners, so it forms a parcel, or purse, with no gaps (see overleaf). Make sure there is no air in the parcel by pressing slowly and carefully on the edges, squeezing out any unwanted air.

Place the filled saccottini on a tray lined with baking paper generously dusted with semolina flour. Place the tray in the fridge and leave for a couple of hours; this will dry out the pasta and give the pasta a better bite when you cook it.

Carefully add the saccottini to a pan of boiling salted water and cook for 3 minutes. Melt the butter in a warm frying pan. Remove the cooked saccottini with a slotted spoon and place in the frying pan with the butter. Add a ladleful of the pasta cooking water and gently cook for a couple of minutes, moving the pan continually so the starch from the pasta and butter emulsify. Serve in warm pasta bowls with some black pepper.

Pictured overleaf

ARTICHOKES

Linguine with violet artichokes

Serves 4 as a starter

4 violet artichokes
juice of 1 lemon
4 tbsp extra-virgin olive oil
1 garlic clove, finely sliced
100ml (3½fl oz) dry white wine
100ml (3½fl oz) water
400g (14oz) dried linguine
16 taggiasche or niçoise
  olives, pitted and roughly
  chopped
25g (1oz) miniature capers
  in vinegar, drained
100g (3½oz) wild rocket
  (arugula), roughly chopped
sea salt and freshly ground
  black pepper

For the pangrattato
2 slices of good-quality,
  dry bread
4 tbsp extra-virgin olive oil
1 tsp thyme leaves

We have had this dish on and off our menu at the restaurant for a long time. It is a real hit with vegans and non-vegans alike, as the artichokes have a lot of flavour and texture and the salty olives, capers and crispy garlicky breadcrumbs make it a very well-balanced pasta.

Take your time when preparing the artichokes – the more care you take, the better they will taste. And the fresher the artichoke, the easier it is to prepare, as the leaves are soft and the choke is firm. A good tip – put the un-prepped artichokes into a sink of cold water and leave them to firm up for 20 minutes to make them easier to prepare.

For the pangrattato, whiz the bread to fine crumbs in a food processor. Add the olive oil to a hot saucepan, add the thyme, then add the breadcrumbs and cook over a low heat, stirring all the time. When the breadcrumbs are evenly golden brown, tip onto a piece of kitchen paper to absorb the excess oil, sprinkle with salt and leave to one side.

Peel off the outer dark green leaves of an artichoke to reveal the tender, paler leaves. Using a swivel potato peeler, peel the tough outer fibrous stem of the artichoke until the tender part is revealed. Cut the pointed tips off by 5cm (2in). Using a teaspoon, scoop out the thistly centre piece of the artichoke and place in some water with the lemon juice added. Repeat with the remaining artichokes and leave for 10 minutes to soak, so they don't oxidize.

Cut the artichokes in half lengthways through the stem and heart and then lay cut side down on a chopping board and cut each half into 5 thin slices.

In a hot, large non-stick frying pan add 2 tablespoons of the olive oil, the garlic, artichoke slices, white wine and water. Place a lid on top and cook over a medium heat for 10 minutes, until the artichokes are tender – check with a small, sharp knife. Take off the heat and leave to one side.

Cook the linguine in a large pan of boiling salted water for 3 minutes less than the packet suggests. Place the frying pan with the cooked artichokes back over a medium heat. Remove the linguine using a pair of tongs and add it to the artichoke pan, with a couple of ladlefuls of pasta water. Turn up the heat so the liquid starts to reduce, and wiggle the pan to toss and combine. Add the olives, capers, rocket and remaining 2 tablespoons of olive oil and toss again, cooking for a couple more minutes. Check the seasoning, then serve in warm bowls, sprinkled generously with the pangrattato and some black pepper.

Salad of artichoke hearts, potatoes, dandelion and celery leaves

Serves 4

600g (1lb 5oz) Ratte (or any
  waxy) potatoes, skins on
  and thoroughly washed
8 small violet artichokes (use
  jarred if you can't get fresh –
  wash and dry them first)
1 lemon, halved
1kg (2lb 3oz) wild dandelion
  bunches still on the root
  (you want about 3 generous
  handfuls of leaves)
2 tbsp red wine vinegar
75g (2½oz) pine nuts
12 taggiasche olives, pitted
  and chopped
10 caper berries, halved
1 tbsp chopped flat-leaf
  parsley
1 tbsp honey
5 tbsp extra-virgin olive oil
handful of celery leaves
sea salt and freshly ground
  black pepper

Artichokes come in all shapes and sizes and each one has
a culinary purpose. The little ones are best boiled, peeled
and marinated. If you can't find small, fresh artichokes you
can use ones from a jar – just make sure you wash off the jar
marinade first, as it tends to be very vinegary and heavy with
sunflower oil.

Dandelion grows wild almost everywhere. So take a small
trowel or, better still, a garden fork and dig up the nicest
looking dandelions you can find.

Add the potatoes to a large pan of cold salted water, bring to
a simmer and cook over a medium heat for about 30 minutes,
until tender. Drain and leave to cool down. When cool, halve
lengthways and leave to one side.

If using fresh artichokes, place the artichokes and lemon halves
in a saucepan and fill to the top with cold water. Add a pinch of
salt and place a smaller lid on top of the artichokes to keep them
submerged. Cook over a medium heat for about 25 minutes.
Check the artichokes are fully cooked by pushing the point of a
sharp knife through the stem and heart: if there is no resistance,
they are cooked. Carefully remove the artichokes from the water
to cool. When cool, peel off the outer leaves to reveal the young,
tender leaves. Peel off the tough stringy outside of the stem
and cut off the sharp tips. Halve lengthways and then, using
a teaspoon, scoop out the thistly choke. Leave the prepared
artichokes to one side. Omit this step if using jarred artichokes.

Remove the roots, then thoroughly wash the dandelions to
remove any mud. Using a pair of scissors, snip off the smaller,
lighter leaves, discarding any withered or tough-looking leaves.
Soak the tender leaves for 30 minutes in a big bowlful of water
combined with a capful of Milton disinfectant. Drain and rinse
thoroughly in cold water.

Add the dandelion leaves to a pan of boiling salted water
and cook for 3–4 minutes. Drain and leave to cool down in a
colander. Place the cooked dandelion on some kitchen paper,
press down and squeeze to extract all the moisture. If they are
not completely dried, then the salad will be watery.

Add the vinegar, pine nuts, olives, caper berries, parsley, honey
and olive oil to a large bowl. Whisk all the ingredients thoroughly
so the dressing becomes emulsified. Add the potatoes to the
bowl and mix, then add the artichokes, tossing carefully, so as
not to break them. Mix through the dandelion and celery leaves,
then check the seasoning. Serve in a large bowl at the table.

Artichoke and porcini risotto

Serves 4 as a starter

4 violet artichokes
juice of 1 lemon
2 tbsp extra-virgin olive oil
1 garlic clove, finely sliced
100ml (3½fl oz) dry white wine
100ml (3½fl oz) water
sea salt and freshly ground
 black pepper

For the risotto
2 tbsp extra-virgin olive oil
1 tsp thyme leaves
1 onion, finely chopped
3 tbsp finely chopped celery
250g (9oz) Carnaroli
 risotto rice
20g (¾oz) dried porcini,
 soaked in hot water for
 15 minutes, drained and
 finely chopped
1 garlic clove, crushed to
 a paste with a little sea salt
1 tbsp chopped flat-leaf
 parsley
½ lemon
75g (2½oz) butter
75g (2½oz) mascarpone
150g (5½oz) parmesan,
 grated, plus extra to serve

For the vegetable stock
2 carrots, peeled and
 roughly chopped
1 leek, roughly chopped
2 celery stalks, roughly
 chopped
1 tsp sea salt
3 litres (105fl oz) water

I love a good risotto, and porcini and artichokes are two of my favourite ingredients. They are both earthy, but mixed with the creamy mascarpone and parmesan, make a terrific risotto. Always serve this straight from the pot at the table in warm bowls.

Make the stock. Place all the ingredients in a large saucepan, bring to the boil, then turn down the heat and simmer for 1 hour. Strain into a second pan and return the liquid to a low heat.

Peel off the outer dark green leaves of an artichoke to reveal the tender, paler leaves. Using a swivel potato peeler, peel the tough outer fibrous stem of the artichoke until the tender part is revealed. Cut the pointed tips off by 5cm (2in). Using a teaspoon, scoop out the thistly centre piece of the artichoke and place in some water with the lemon juice added. Repeat with the remaining artichokes and leave for 10 minutes to soak, so they don't oxidize.

Halve the artichokes lengthways through the stem, lay them cut side down on a chopping board and cut each half into 5 slices.

Add the oil to a hot, large non-stick frying pan, and add the garlic, artichoke slices, white wine and water. Place a lid on top and cook over a medium heat for 10 minutes, until the artichokes are tender. Take off the heat and leave to one side.

To make the risotto, add the olive oil to a hot, straight-sided saucepan, then add the thyme, onion and celery. Cook for 2 minutes, then add the rice and cook gently for 5 minutes, stirring occasionally with a wooden spoon, so the rice becomes slightly translucent. Add a ladleful of the hot vegetable stock and stir, repeating this process until the rice still has a bite but is not crunchy, about 15 minutes. The risotto should be very wet at this stage, almost soupy.

Add the cooked artichokes and any excess cooking liquid, along with the porcini. Stir well, then add the crushed garlic in salt, parsley and a squeeze of lemon. Check the rice has a bite to it but not too much. Take off the heat and add the butter, mascarpone and parmesan. Stir vigorously so the risotto becomes emulsified. Place a tight-fitting lid on top and leave for 2 minutes. This will steam the rice grains in their own liquid, releasing more starch and making the risotto even creamier. Stir again thoroughly and serve in warm bowls with black pepper and some more parmesan.

Artichoke dip with crispy farinata

Serves 8 as a snack

For the artichoke dip
2 x 400g (14oz) cans of
   artichoke hearts, drained
1 garlic clove, crushed to
   a paste with a little sea salt
1 tbsp chopped flat-leaf
   parsley
50g (1¾oz) parmesan, grated
juice of 1 lemon
100g (3½oz) wild rocket
   (arugula)
75ml (2¼fl oz) extra-virgin
   olive oil
sea salt and freshly ground
   black pepper

For the farinata
400g (14oz) chickpea
   (gram) flour
50ml (1¾fl oz) extra-virgin
   olive oil, plus extra for frying
800ml (27fl oz) warm water
1 tsp finely chopped rosemary
1 tsp fine sea salt

This is a tasty and very simple dip to make, requiring little work. Canned artichokes are whizzed to a dip in a blender with parmesan, lemon juice and olive oil – it couldn't be simpler. The farinata is a chickpea pancake fried in olive oil and sprinkled with salt. There is no gluten in chickpeas so this is perfect for anyone with a gluten intolerance. Simply tear, dip and scoop the farinata with the dip on the side, or roll the dip inside the pancakes for easy eating – perfect with an aperitivo.

Place all the ingredients for the artichoke dip, with salt and black pepper to taste, in a food processor and blitz for 2–3 minutes, until smooth. Check the seasoning and place in a nice serving bowl. Place in the fridge, until ready to serve.

Place the chickpea flour in a large bowl and make a well in the middle. Add the olive oil to the well, then slowly pour in the warm water, whisking so the water and oil start to combine smoothly. When you have added all the water you should have a batter that easily coats the back of a spoon. Add the rosemary, whisk again, then cover with cling film (plastic wrap) and place in the fridge for 1 hour.

Add 1 tablespoon of oil to a hot, large non-stick frying pan. Move the oil all over the pan so the base is covered. Take a large ladle of the chickpea batter and place it in the centre of the pan. Tilt the pan so the batter spreads all over the base. Cook over a medium heat for 3 minutes, then give the pan a good shake and the pancake should loosen. Flip the pancake, then cook for a further 3 minutes on the other side. Once both sides are golden, place on a wire rack and sprinkle with a little fine salt. Repeat until you have cooked all the chickpea pancakes, adding a tablespoon of olive oil each time. Don't stack the pancakes on top of each other or they will go soggy.

To serve them my preferred way, place a chickpea pancake on a plate, take a generous spoonful of the artichoke dip and spread evenly onto the chickpea pancake. Roll the pancake up like a cigar to eat. Alternatively, serve the pancakes and dip in the middle of the table for everyone to tear and scoop.

Globe and Jerusalem artichoke soup with black truffle crostini

Serves 4

4 violet artichokes
juice of 1 lemon
400g (14oz) peeled Jerusalem
  artichokes
4 tbsp extra-virgin olive oil,
  plus extra for drizzling
2 medium leeks, cut into
  1cm (½in) rounds
2 medium potatoes, peeled
  and cut into 3cm (1¼in)
  pieces
1 tsp thyme leaves
2 litres (68fl oz) vegetable
  stock (see page 19 for
  homemade)
100ml (3½fl oz) double
  (heavy) cream
1 tbsp chopped flat-leaf
  parsley
1 small ciabatta loaf
75ml (2¼fl oz) crème fraîche
1 egg yolk
50g (1¾oz) parmesan,
  finely grated
20g (¾oz) black truffle,
  finely grated
sea salt and freshly ground
  black pepper

Jerusalem artichokes are very different to globe artichokes, but they are wonderful when cooked together. If you can get hold of some black truffle, the soup and crostini will taste even better; black truffle and Jerusalem artichokes are made for each other.

Peel off the outer dark green leaves of an artichoke to reveal the tender, paler leaves. Using a swivel potato peeler, peel the tough outer fibrous stem of the artichoke until the tender part is revealed. Cut the pointed tips off by 5cm (2in). Using a teaspoon, scoop out the thistly centre piece of the artichoke and place in some water with the lemon juice added. Repeat with the remaining artichokes and leave for 10 minutes to soak, so they don't oxidize.

Halve the artichokes lengthways through the stem, lay them cut side down on a chopping board and cut each half into 5 slices.

Halve the peeled Jerusalem artichokes, then roughly chop them. Place them in a bowl and cover with cold water.

Add the oil to a hot, large saucepan, then add the drained violet and Jerusalem artichokes and 1 teaspoon of salt. Cook over a medium heat for 10 minutes, so the artichokes start to get a little colour. Add the leeks, potatoes and thyme, then the stock. Bring to the boil, turn down the heat and simmer for 40 minutes. All the vegetables should be well cooked, and the potatoes should be soft. If the soup feels a bit thick, thin it with a cup or two of boiled water from the kettle. Using a balloon whisk, mash the soup up a bit, then add the cream and parsley and bring to a simmer. Check the seasoning, place a lid on top, remove from the heat and keep warm. It's always a good idea to rest a soup for a few minutes before you serve it.

While the soup is cooking, preheat the oven to 180°C/160°C fan/ 350°F/Gas 4.

Slice the ciabatta at an angle and place 4 generous slices on a roasting tray. Drizzle with olive oil and sprinkle with a pinch of salt. Bake in the oven for 4 minutes.

In a bowl, mix the crème fraîche, egg yolk, parmesan and black truffle together. Divide the mixture between the 4 crostini and place back in the oven for 5 minutes. The crème fraîche mixture should be set and be slightly coloured.

Serve the soup in warm bowls with a baked crostini on the side.

Globe artichoke, leek, fennel, broccoli and radicchio salad

Serves 4 as a starter

12 baby leeks, trimmed
2 fennel bulbs, cut into
  1cm (½in) slices
500g (1lb 2oz) tenderstem
  broccoli, tough ends
  removed
1 x 400g (14oz) jar of
  best-quality grilled
  artichokes, drained
1 radicchio head, bitter
  outer leaves removed
100g (3½oz) roasted, salted
  almonds (see page 62)
sea salt and freshly ground
  black pepper

For the dressing
1 garlic clove, peeled
½ tsp sea salt
1 tsp thyme leaves
1 tbsp honey
2 tbsp white wine vinegar
juice of 1 clementine
5 tbsp extra-virgin olive oil

I have used grilled artichokes from a jar for this recipe but if you have fresh artichokes, then all you need to do is boil them, peel off the tough outer leaves, scoop out the choke and cut them in half lengthways (see page 90). Place them flat-side down on a hot griddle pan so they have char marks, then mix with olive oil and lemon juice.

This is a salad full of flavour and texture – the sweetness from the honey and clementine works beautifully with the charred vegetables, bitter leaves and the crunch of salty almonds. Perfect as part of an antipasti spread.

Add the leeks to a large pan of boiling salted water and cook for 5 minutes until tender. Take out using a pair of tongs and place on a tray lined with kitchen paper to drain. Add the fennel to the same water and cook for 4 minutes, until soft. Take out with a slotted spoon and place on kitchen paper. Add the tenderstem broccoli to the same water and cook for 4 minutes, then drain into a colander and leave to cool.

Heat a non-stick frying pan or griddle pan until very hot. Place the fennel slices on the griddle pan so they get a light char on the outside. Do the same with the leeks and the tenderstem broccoli. Once you have grilled all the vegetables, cut each leek into 3 pieces and cut the broccoli in half lengthways. Keep them all to one side.

To make the dressing, in a pestle and mortar, pound the garlic, salt and thyme to a smooth paste. Add the honey, vinegar, clementine juice and oil. Mix well so the dressing is emulsified.

Add the dressing to a large bowl, then add the grilled artichokes, leeks, broccoli and fennel, and the radicchio leaves and roasted almonds. Mix so all the ingredients are coated in the dressing. Add black pepper and check the seasoning. Serve on a platter or divide between small plates.

Fritto misto of globe and Jerusalem artichokes with walnut pesto

Serves 4 as snack

4 violet artichokes
juice of 1 lemon, plus 4 lemon
  wedges, to serve
500g (1lb 2oz) peeled
  Jerusalem artichokes, cut
  into 1cm (½in) slices
500ml (17fl oz) whole milk
500g (1lb 2oz) tipo 00 flour
500ml (17fl oz) sunflower oil
sea salt and freshly ground
  black pepper

For the walnut pesto
1 garlic clove, peeled
½ tsp sea salt
100g (3½oz) walnuts
4 tbsp milk
100g (3½oz) parmesan, grated
juice of ½ lemon
4 tbsp extra-virgin olive oil
50g (1¾oz) breadcrumbs
1 tbsp chopped flat-leaf
  parsley

The best deep-fried globe artichokes tend to be the ones you make at home, especially if you have really fresh ones. I've found Jerusalem artichokes cooked this way taste delicious too – try and cut them no thicker than 1cm (½in) or they might be a little crunchy. This is very simple to make, as there is no batter. The walnut pesto is a nice additional flavour and perfect to dip the crisp artichokes in.

Make the walnut pesto. Place the garlic and salt in a pestle and mortar and crush to a fine paste, then add the walnuts and pound until smooth. Add the milk and grind until the sauce has emulsified, then add the parmesan, lemon juice and olive oil. Mix so the sauce is smooth and well combined, then stir in the breadcrumbs and parsley so you have a thick-set sauce that looks a bit like hummus.

Peel off the outer dark green leaves of an artichoke to reveal the tender, paler leaves. Using a swivel potato peeler, peel the tough outer fibrous stem of the artichoke until the tender part is revealed. Cut the pointed tips off by 5cm (2in). Using a teaspoon, scoop out the thistly centre piece of the artichoke and place in some water with the lemon juice added. Repeat with the remaining artichokes and leave for 10 minutes to soak, so they don't oxidize.

Halve the artichokes lengthways through the stem, lay them cut side down on a chopping board and cut each half into 4 wedges. Place the artichoke wedges back in the lemon water.

Place the violet and Jerusalem artichokes in a bowl with the milk and leave to soak for 5 minutes. Take them out of the milk with a slotted spoon and transfer them to a bowl or tray along with the flour. With your hands, toss the artichokes with the flour so they are completely coated.

To fry the artichokes, heat the oil in a large frying pan until it reads 170°C/325°F on a cooking thermometer, or test by adding a piece of artichoke: if it sizzles immediately, the oil is hot enough. Fry the artichokes in batches until golden brown. Remove with a slotted spoon and place on a wire rack with a tray underneath to catch excess oil.

Sprinkle the fried artichokes with salt and serve on starter plates, with the walnut pesto on the side and lemon wedges for squeezing.

Jerusalem artichoke frittata with fontina and black truffle

Serves 4

3 tbsp extra-virgin olive oil
1 medium onion, thinly sliced
½ tsp thyme leaves
400g (14oz) peeled Jerusalem
  artichokes, thinly sliced
6 eggs
75ml (2¼fl oz) milk
150g (5½oz) fontina, grated
1 tbsp chopped flat-leaf
  parsley
50g (1¾oz) unsalted butter
20g (¾oz) black truffle
  (optional)
sea salt and freshly ground
  black pepper

If you can get hold of a black truffle, then this is a great recipe to use it in. I first had this combination in Switzerland back in 2008 and the flavours have stuck with me ever since. Jerusalem artichokes taste best when they are braised and their sugars start releasing. They eventually go soft and (being a root vegetable and therefore naturally sweet) slightly caramelized, which gives them a lovely nutty taste on top of all the other flavours that they're able to absorb. Fontina works well but if you can't find any, substitute it with Gruyère.

Add the oil to a hot, large, non-stick, ovenproof frying pan, then add the onion and thyme and cook for 3 minutes over a medium heat. Add the sliced Jerusalem artichokes and a good pinch of salt. Place the lid on and cook for 20 minutes, stirring occasionally to make sure the artichokes don't stick and get too much colour. When the artichokes are soft and you can put a knife through one without any resistance, take them out of the pan and leave to cool down.

Meanwhile, preheat the oven to 180°C/160°C fan/350°F/Gas 4.

In a large bowl, whisk the eggs and milk with some salt and black pepper until well combined. Add the cooled cooked Jerusalem artichokes, the fontina and parsley, and mix well.

Wipe out the frying pan you cooked the Jerusalem artichokes in and place over a medium heat. Add the butter and, when it has melted and starts to foam, tilt the pan to coat the base and sides. Pour in the frittata mixture and wiggle the pan so the mixture comes away slightly from the sides. After 3 minutes, place the pan in the oven and cook for a further 4 minutes or until the egg has set and there is a little colour on top of the frittata.

Take out of the oven and leave to one side for a few minutes. When ready to serve, put the frying pan back over the heat for 1 minute. Then, using a plate slightly bigger than the circumference of the pan, carefully invert the frittata onto the plate. Grate over the truffle, if using. Serve as a starter or as a light main course with a crisp green salad.

Jerusalem and globe artichoke salad

Serves 4 as a starter or side

200g (7oz) peeled Jerusalem
    artichokes
4 heritage carrots
4 celery stalks
6 red radishes
2 fennel bulbs, fronds
    reserved
2 violet artichokes
juice of 1 lemon
8 mint leaves
80g (3oz) walnuts
150g (5½oz) parmesan

For the dressing
juice of 1 lemon
4 tbsp extra-virgin olive oil
1 tbsp honey
25g (1oz) miniature capers
    in vinegar, drained
sea salt and freshly ground
    black pepper

A decent mandoline is essential for this salad, but use a guard as this will avoid any accidents. It's very important to place the vegetables in iced water before and after you slice them on the mandoline, as this will make them easier to slice and the salad crisper. This may seem like a very simple salad, but it's full of crunch and freshness.

Place the Jerusalem artichokes, carrots, celery, radishes and fennel in a large bowl of iced water.

Peel off the outer dark green leaves of a violet artichoke to reveal the tender, paler leaves. Using a swivel potato peeler, peel the tough outer fibrous stem of the artichoke until the tender part is revealed. Cut the pointed tips off by 5cm (2in). Using a teaspoon, scoop out the thistly centre piece of the artichoke and place in some water with the lemon juice added. Repeat with the remaining artichoke and leave for 10 minutes to soak, so they don't oxidize.

Halve the artichokes lengthways through the stem, lay them cut side down on a chopping board and slice each half as thinly as possible. Place the artichoke slices back in the lemon water.

Using a mandoline, finely slice the Jerusalem artichokes, carrots, celery, radishes and fennel. Return the sliced vegetables to the bowl of iced water.

Mix the dressing ingredients together in a large bowl, using a balloon whisk to emulsify it.

Drain off the soaking water from the Jerusalem artichokes, carrots, celery, radish and fennel. Do the same with the globe artichokes and, in batches, spin all the vegetables in a salad spinner so they are dry but crisp.

Add the sliced vegetables, the mint and fennel fronds to the dressing bowl and toss well so the dressing coats all the vegetables. Check the seasoning and tip into a serving bowl. Scatter with the walnuts and, using a swivel potato peeler, shave parmesan over the top.

Farfalle, lentils and Jerusalem artichokes with crème fraîche

Serves 4

100g (3½oz) dried Umbrian
   or Puy (French) lentils
3 tbsp extra-virgin olive oil
1 medium carrot, finely
   chopped
3 celery stalks, finely chopped
1 medium onion, finely
   chopped
1 tsp thyme leaves
300g (10½oz) peeled
   Jerusalem artichokes,
   finely sliced
150ml (5fl oz) crème fraîche
400g (14oz) dried farfalle
1 tbsp chopped flat-leaf
   parsley
100g (3½oz) parmesan,
   grated, plus extra to serve
sea salt and freshly ground
   black pepper

This may not be a colourful pasta, but it tastes great and is perfect for a cold evening. Farfalle, or butterfly, pasta is the perfect shape for this sauce, as it holds the lentils and the cooked creamy artichoke sauce perfectly. Farfalle pasta comes from the northern Italian region of Emilia-Romagna, home to so many great ingredients, including parmesan.

Add the lentils to a small saucepan and add water to come 5cm (2in) above the level of the lentils. Cook for 20 minutes or until tender and with a little bite. Drain and put to one side.

Add the oil to a hot, large non-stick frying pan, then add the carrot, celery, onion, ½ teaspoon of salt and the thyme. Cook over a medium heat for 5 minutes, add the sliced Jerusalem artichokes, then place a lid on the pan and leave to cook for 10 minutes. Push a knife through the thickest part of the Jerusalem artichoke and if it goes through with no resistance then the artichoke is cooked. Add the drained lentils and the crème fraîche, turn the heat down to low and cook for 5 minutes.

Meanwhile, add the farfalle to a large saucepan of boiling salted water and cook for 3 minutes less than the packet suggests. Using a slotted spoon or small sieve, take out the pasta and place in the frying pan with the artichoke sauce. Put the frying pan back over a medium heat and add 2 ladlefuls of the pasta cooking water. Cook for 3 minutes, stirring with a wooden spoon so the pasta and sauce start to combine and the starch from the pasta thickens the sauce.

Add the chopped parsley, and finally the parmesan. Check the seasoning, and if the pasta feels a little dry, add some more pasta water.

Serve in warm bowls, with a little extra parmesan on top.

MUSHROOMS

Funghi ripieni

**Serves 4 as a starter
or lunch**

8 large portobello mushrooms,
  stems removed and reserved
2 tbsp extra-virgin olive oil
1 tsp thyme leaves
100g (3½oz) dried
  breadcrumbs
100g (3½oz) parmesan,
  grated
1 garlic clove, crushed to
  a paste with a little sea salt
100g (3½oz) soft butter
2 tbsp chopped flat-leaf
  parsley
1 lemon, cut into quarters,
  to serve
sea salt and freshly ground
  black pepper

**Stuffed and baked mushrooms are simple to make and
are very tasty. I have used portobello here but any flat cap
mushroom will do. The garlicky butter and parmesan really
make the dish, so don't hold back if you want to add more.
It's important that the mushrooms are cooked through and
not too firm, so if you feel they need a bit longer in the oven,
then put them in for another 5 minutes.**

**These are lovely as a lunch dish or starter, mopped up with
some toasted ciabatta.**

Preheat the oven to 180°C/160°C fan/350°F/Gas 4.

In a large bowl, carefully toss the mushroom caps with the olive
oil, thyme and some salt and black pepper, so each mushroom is
lightly coated in olive oil. Place them on a baking tray, open cap
facing upwards, cook in the oven for 10 minutes, then remove.

Add the breadcrumbs, parmesan, crushed garlic in salt, butter
and parsley to the bowl you mixed the mushrooms in. Finely
chop the stems from the portobello mushrooms and add to
the bowl, mixing to combine all the ingredients. Check the
seasoning; you will probably only need black pepper as the
salt from crushing the garlic will be enough.

Divide the filling mixture equally between the mushroom caps,
carefully placing it into each so the tops are evenly covered.
Cook in the oven for 10 minutes, then serve immediately with
a squeeze of lemon.

Mushroom, cauliflower and Jerusalem artichoke soup

Serves 4

3 tbsp extra-virgin olive oil,
  plus extra for greasing
  and drizzling
800g (1lb 12oz) cauliflower,
  cut into roughly 8 pieces
6 banana shallots, peeled
  and halved lengthways
300g (10½oz) peeled
  Jerusalem artichokes, sliced
400g (14oz) chestnut (cremini)
  mushrooms, quartered
300g (10½oz) peeled Désirée
  or Cyprus potatoes, cut into
  roughly 3cm (1¼in) pieces
1 tsp thyme leaves
2 litres (68fl oz) vegetable
  stock (see page 19 for
  homemade)
150ml (5fl oz) double
  (heavy) cream
1 tbsp chopped flat-leaf
  parsley
4 generous slices of ciabatta
100g (3½oz) fontina or
  Gruyère, grated
sea salt and freshly ground
  black pepper

Roasting the vegetables here makes a big difference to the flavour of the finished soup, and sealing the roasting tin with foil allows the vegetables to steam and cook through properly. Roasted shallots have a sweet and nutty flavour, which, combined with the addition of cream, makes for a rich and luxurious soup. The fontina crostini is so good with the soup – don't skip it.

Preheat the oven to 180°C/160°C fan/350°F/Gas 4.

Rub the insides of a roasting tin with olive oil, then add the cauliflower, shallots, Jerusalem artichokes, mushrooms, potatoes, thyme, and some salt and black pepper. Mix all the ingredients so they are coated in oil, then tightly cover with baking paper and a layer of foil. Cook in the oven for 35 minutes, then take off the foil and baking paper and put back in the oven for a further 5 minutes, so the moisture can evaporate and concentrate the flavour. Remove from the oven and transfer the roasted vegetables to a large saucepan, making sure you scrape everything from the roasting tin.

Place the saucepan over a medium heat and pour in the vegetable stock. Bring to the boil, then turn down the heat and simmer for 25 minutes, then remove from the heat. Using a stick blender, blitz the soup until smooth. If the soup feels a bit too thick, add more stock, or water from the kettle. Add the cream and parsley and cook for a further 5 minutes over a low heat. Check the seasoning.

Place the ciabatta slices on a roasting tray, drizzle with olive oil and bake in the oven for 5 minutes. Take out of the oven, place a generous amount of grated cheese on each ciabatta toast, then place back in the oven until the cheese has melted and has a little colour.

Serve the soup in bowls with the fontina crostini on the side.

Mushroom, onion and spinach torta

Serves 4 for lunch

1 x 320g (11¼oz) sheet
   of ready-rolled all-butter
   puff pastry
flour, for dusting
1 egg, plus an extra egg
   beaten with 1 tbsp milk
   for egg wash
4 tbsp extra-virgin olive oil
1 tsp thyme leaves
600g (1lb 5oz) chestnut
   (cremini) mushrooms, sliced
4 red onions, finely sliced
400g (14oz) spinach leaves,
   blanched in boiling water
   and squeezed so there is
   no excess water
100ml (3½fl oz) crème fraîche
75g (2½oz) parmesan, grated
sea salt and freshly ground
   black pepper

This recipe is super-easy to make, as it uses shop-bought puff pastry. The sweet onions give it a lovely flavour and the drizzle of crème fraîche, egg and parmesan on top holds everything together, while also adding richness to the tart. Serve as a canapé cut into small pieces, or with a salad for lunch.

Preheat the oven to 180°C/160°C fan/350°F/Gas 4.

Place the puff pastry sheet on a roasting tray with a little flour underneath to prevent it from sticking. Using a pastry brush, paint the egg wash on the top side of the puff pastry so the entire surface is coated. Place in the oven for 20 minutes, until risen and a nice golden brown colour. Take the tray out of the oven and place on a wire rack to cool.

Add 2 tablespoons of the olive oil to a hot, large non-stick frying pan, then add the thyme, mushrooms and some salt and black pepper. Cook over a medium heat for 20 minutes, until the mushrooms are dark and sticky and the flavour is concentrated. Keep the mushrooms to one side.

Add the remaining 2 tablespoons of olive oil to a hot saucepan, and add the red onions with some salt and black pepper. Cook over a medium heat for 20 minutes, stirring occasionally, until soft and slightly caramelized.

Spread the cooked onions over the cooled pastry sheet, then scatter the mushrooms over the onions in an even layer. Chop the cooked and squeezed spinach and scatter on top of the mushrooms and onions.

In a small bowl, beat the egg with a fork and stir in the crème fraîche, parmesan and some salt and black pepper. Beat thoroughly so all the ingredients are combined, then drizzle it all over the spinach, mushrooms and onions.

Bake in the oven for 20 minutes until the top is lightly golden all over, then place on a wire rack and leave for 10 minutes before serving.

Serve as a canapé in small squares, or as a tasty lunch dish with a green salad on the side.

Green mushroom lasagne

Serves 4

2 tbsp extra-virgin olive oil
250g (9oz) smoked scamorza,
    finely sliced
sea salt and freshly ground
    black pepper

For the green pasta dough
350g (12oz) tipo 00 flour
25g (1oz) fine semolina flour,
    plus extra for dusting
1 egg, plus 4 egg yolks
100g (3½oz) baby spinach,
    blanched in boiling water,
    drained, squeezed and
    finely chopped

For the filling
3 tbsp extra-virgin olive oil
1 tsp thyme leaves
300g (10½oz) portobello
    mushrooms, cut into 5mm
    (¼in) slices
400g (14oz) chestnut (cremini)
    mushrooms, cut into 5mm
    (¼in) slices
20g (¾oz) dried porcini
    mushrooms, soaked in
    500ml (17fl oz) hot water
    for 15 minutes
2 medium leeks, sliced into
    1cm (½in) rounds

For the béchamel
50g (1¾oz) butter
40g (1½oz) plain
    (all-purpose) flour
500ml (17fl oz) hot milk
100g (3½oz) parmesan, grated
250g (9oz) ricotta

My mother once entered a cookery competition for Lurpak butter, and made a leek and mushroom fresh pasta roll. I had just started working at The River Café, so she got me to taste her creation a few times to make sure it was tip top... well it was, and she won the first prize of an all-expenses-paid trip to Australia. I always think of her dish whenever I combine mushrooms and leeks in a recipe.

The smoked scamorza cheese adds an extra flavour, which works well with the mushrooms and leeks.

To make the green pasta dough, place all the ingredients in a food processor and blitz for 1 minute. Make sure everything is combining well, then continue to blitz until the dough turns pale green. Take out the pasta dough and divide in half, wrap in cling film (plastic wrap) and place in the fridge for 20 minutes.

Remove the pasta dough from the fridge and, using a rolling pin or pasta machine, roll out into long sheets; when you can see the silhouette of your hand behind the pasta, then it is the correct thickness.

Cut the pasta into 5 sheets the length and width of the dish you want to make the lasagne in. Place on a flat tray dusted with fine semolina flour, with a piece of baking paper and another dusting of fine semolina flour between each sheet. Leave to dry for 45 minutes while you make the filling and béchamel.

For the filling, add 1 tablespoon of the olive oil to a hot, large non-stick frying pan, then add the thyme, followed by the sliced portobello and chestnut mushrooms. Season with salt and black pepper and cook for 15 minutes over a medium heat, until the mushrooms have become dark and sticky. Remove the porcini from their soaking liquid, chop and add to the mushroom pan. Strain the soaking liquid through some kitchen paper or a paper coffee filter, to remove any grit, then pour into the frying pan. Cook until the porcini water has reduced and the mushrooms are dark and concentrated.

Transfer the mushroom mixture to a bowl and keep to one side. Place the pan back over the heat with the remaining 2 tablespoons of olive oil. Add the leeks and cook down for about 15 minutes, until soft and sweet. Season and mix with the mushrooms, then keep to one side.

Melt the butter for the béchamel in a medium saucepan over a medium heat, then add the flour and cook for 3 minutes, stirring with a wooden spoon. Slowly add the hot milk, stirring continuously to avoid any lumps. When you have added all the milk, leave to cook over a low heat for 15 minutes. Stir in the parmesan and ricotta and leave to cool.

Now it is time to put the lasagne together. Preheat the oven to 180°C/160°C fan/350°F/Gas 4.

Two sheets at a time, blanch the pasta for 1 minute in a pan of boiling salted water, then remove to a bowl of iced water to cool them quickly. Drain all the blanched pasta sheets in a colander and keep to one side.

Add 1 tablespoon of olive oil to the dish you are making the lasagne in, ensuring the inside of the dish is completely coated. Start making the lasagne by laying a sheet of pasta in the bottom and then add a quarter of the leek and mushroom mixture, making sure it is evenly spread. Add about a fifth of the béchamel, then place a sheet of pasta on top and repeat until you have 4 layers. Top with the final pasta sheet, then pour over the remaining béchamel and arrange the smoked scamorza on top in a single layer.

Rub a large sheet of foil with the remaining tablespoon of olive oil, then (oil side down) tightly cover the lasagne. Cook in the oven for 35 minutes, then remove the foil and cook for a further 10 minutes, or until the lasagne is a light golden-brown colour and crispy at the edges. Leave to rest and cool for 15 minutes before serving; this will allow the moisture to be absorbed into the pasta and will make it easier to serve. Serve in warm pasta bowls, with black pepper.

Pictured overleaf

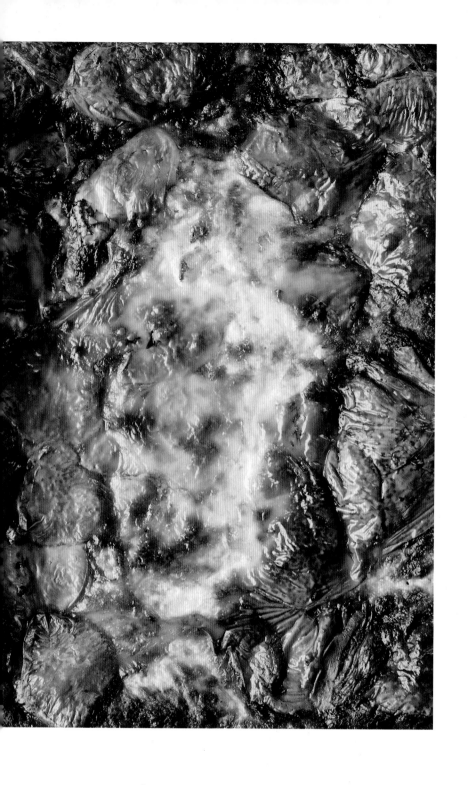

Baked gnocchi with porcini, tomatoes and smoked scamorza

Serves 4

20g (¾oz) dried porcini
 mushrooms, soaked in
 500ml (17fl oz) hot water
 for 15 minutes
3 tbsp extra-virgin olive oil,
 plus extra for the dish
1 garlic clove, finely sliced
1 tsp thyme leaves
600ml (20fl oz) tomato passata
 (strained tomatoes)
500g (1lb 2oz) potato gnocchi
2 tbsp mascarpone
250g (9oz) smoked scamorza,
 finely sliced
sea salt and freshly ground
 black pepper

**Tomato and porcini is a heavenly combination. I have
had this sauce on the menu at the restaurant with fresh
pappardelle for many years and it never disappoints, but
when I tried it with gnocchi and baked it with smoked
scamorza on top, I realized this was a great variation.**

**I have used shop-bought gnocchi here because they hold
together well, especially as they are boiled then baked.
This is a real winter warmer and is very filling, perfect for
cold, dark evenings.**

Preheat the oven to 180°C/160°C fan/350°F/Gas 4.

Remove the porcini from their soaking liquid, finely chop and
set aside. Strain the soaking water through some kitchen paper
or a paper coffee filter to remove any grit and leave to one side.

Add the olive oil to a hot, large, non-stick frying pan, then add
the garlic and thyme and cook for 1 minute, without letting the
garlic take on any colour. Add the chopped porcini and the
strained soaking liquid and reduce the liquid by half before
adding the passata. Cook slowly for 15 minutes, or until reduced
by half. Keep warm.

Cook the gnocchi in a pan of boiling salted water until they rise
to the top of the pan, then cook for a further minute. Remove with
a slotted spoon and add to the tomato and porcini mushroom
sauce, along with a ladleful of gnocchi cooking water. Add the
mascarpone and cook for 2–3 minutes over a medium heat,
stirring with a wooden spoon so everything is nicely combined.
The sauce should be thick enough to coat the back of a spoon
easily. Check the seasoning, take off the heat and leave to one
side for 2 minutes.

Rub the insides of a baking dish with olive oil. Pour in the
gnocchi and sauce and give the dish a shake so the gnocchi
and sauce are even and level. Place the sliced scamorza all over
the top of the gnocchi and transfer it to the oven for 15 minutes.
The scamorza should be melted and have a little colour on it,
and the gnocchi and sauce should be thicker and bubbling.

Serve at the table with a big serving spoon, in warm pasta bowls,
with black pepper on top.

Roast potatoes with portobello and oyster mushrooms

Serves 4 as a side dish

1kg (2lb 3oz) Cyprus or
 Désirée potatoes, peeled
 and cut into roughly 3cm
 (1¼in) pieces
8 garlic cloves, unpeeled
6 tbsp extra-virgin olive oil
1 tsp thyme leaves
400g (14oz) portobello
 mushrooms, sliced
200g (7oz) oyster mushrooms,
 sliced
1 tbsp chopped flat-leaf
 parsley
squeeze of lemon juice
 (optional)
sea salt and freshly ground
 black pepper

This is a simple potato and mushroom dish that is easy to prepare and has bags of flavour. Serve as a side dish or as part of a spread. The potato choice is crucial – they need to be crispy on the outside and fluffy in the middle, so try and use Désirée or Cyprus, or any red-skinned potato. I sometimes have this as a lunch dish with a green salad, with a sharp vinaigrette and a poached egg.

Preheat the oven to 180°C/160°C fan/350°F/Gas 4.

Add the potatoes and garlic cloves to a large pan of salted water, bring to the boil, turn down the heat to low and cook for 5 minutes, until cooked but still firm and not soft. Drain and keep to one side.

Add 3 tablespoons of the olive oil to a hot, large non-stick frying pan, then add the thyme and the sliced mushrooms with some salt and black pepper. Cook for 10 minutes, so the mushrooms lose their water and become sticky and concentrated.

Line a baking tray with baking paper, placing a drop or two of olive oil on the baking tray so the paper sticks. Pour the remaining olive oil over the baking paper, making sure the whole surface area is greased.

Mix the potatoes, garlic, mushrooms and parsley on the lined tray and check the seasoning. Spread the vegetables out so they cook evenly, then roast in the oven for 20 minutes until crisp. The mushrooms will be drier, but the flavour will be great. Add a little salt and a squeeze of lemon, if you want, to serve.

Girolle and leek risotto

Serves 4

3 tbsp extra-virgin olive oil
400g (14oz) girolle
  mushrooms, cleaned
  and halved
1 garlic clove, sliced
1 tsp thyme leaves
2 medium leeks, sliced into
  1cm (½in) rounds
2 celery stalks, finely chopped
1 small onion, finely chopped
350g (12oz) Carnaroli
  risotto rice
100ml (3½fl oz) dry white wine
2 litres (68fl oz) hot vegetable
  stock (see page 19 for
  homemade)
1 tbsp chopped flat-leaf
  parsley
100g (3½oz) butter
100g (3½oz) parmesan,
  grated, plus extra to serve
sea salt and freshly ground
  black pepper

Girolle mushrooms have a distinctive flavour, almost sweet like an apricot. They are my favourite of the early summer wild mushrooms, and seem to be easier to buy these days in smart greengrocers and from online specialists. In fact, the preserved ones from a jar are good too, but make sure you rinse off the brine as it can overpower the flavour of the girolle when cooked. This is a subtle risotto, not a big mushroomy hit, as the sweet leeks and delicate girolles have a lovely light taste, perfect for an early summer supper.

Add 1 tablespoon of the olive oil to a hot, large, straight-sided saucepan, then add the girolle mushrooms and cook until they release all their water. Add the garlic and thyme and season with salt and black pepper. Take out the mushrooms with a spoon and keep to one side. Add the leeks to the same hot pan and cook for 10 minutes until soft and sweet. Take out of the pan and keep to one side.

Add the remaining 2 tablespoons of olive oil to the pan, and add the celery and onion. Cook for 3 minutes, then add the rice and cook for a further 3 minutes so the rice absorbs the olive oil and goes translucent. Add the wine and cook until it is absorbed, then start adding the hot vegetable stock, a ladleful at a time, so the rice is always just covered. Keep doing this for 10 minutes over a medium heat so the rice is bubbling away. Add the cooked leeks and more stock so the risotto is very wet; after 5 minutes, the liquid should be reduced. Add the cooked girolles and the parsley and check the rice has bite but is not crunchy, then stir through the butter and parmesan. Check the seasoning, take off the heat and stir the risotto vigorously. If it feels a bit thick, add another spoonful or two of vegetable stock; risotto should be wet enough to move to the sides of the bowl when you tilt it.

Place a tight-fitting lid on the pan and leave for 2 minutes. Take off the lid, give it a good stir, check the seasoning again and serve in warm bowls with some extra grated parmesan, and black pepper.

Pappardelle with mushroom and root vegetable ragu

Serves 4 as a starter

2 carrots, peeled
2 medium turnips, peeled
2 parsnips, peeled
1 fennel bulb, outer leaves
  removed
1 medium onion, peeled
  and quartered
3 celery stalks
3 tbsp extra-virgin olive oil
1 tsp thyme leaves
400g (14oz) chestnut (cremini)
  mushrooms, finely chopped
150ml (5fl oz) red wine
400ml (14fl oz) tomato passata
  (strained tomatoes)
350g (12oz) fresh egg
  pappardelle
75g (2½oz) butter
sea salt and freshly ground
  black pepper
grated parmesan, to serve

I have to give credit to my brilliant chef friend Phil Howard who made a wonderful vegetable ragu for a charity dinner we cooked together – this dish is inspired by his recipe. He passed the vegetables through a mincer, which gave the root vegetables an even cut, then cooked them in the classic ragu way. If you prefer to chop them by hand, just make sure they are all roughly the same size. The pappardelle works well with the sauce, but by all means experiment with other pastas – I like to use rigatoni too as it holds the sauce well.

Roughly chop the carrots, turnips, parsnips, fennel, onion and celery, place in batches in a food processor and pulse so you get finely chopped vegetables.

Add the olive oil to a hot, large non-stick frying pan, then add the thyme and the finely chopped root vegetables, with a good pinch of salt, and cook over a low heat with the lid on for 15 minutes. Take off the lid, add the chestnut mushrooms and cook for a further 5 minutes so the vegetables and mushrooms are soft and well cooked. Add the red wine, reduce by half, then add the passata and cook slowly for 20 minutes. Season with salt and black pepper, remove from the heat and keep to one side.

Cook the pappardelle in a large pan of boiling salted water for 1 minute less than the packet suggests. Take out the cooked pappardelle with a pair of tongs and add it to the sauce in the frying pan. Put the pan back over the heat and add 2 ladlefuls of the pasta cooking water to the sauce. Place over a low heat, add the butter and carefully stir the pasta with a wooden spoon so the pasta and sauce start to emulsify.

Check the seasoning and serve in warm pasta bowls, sprinkled with grated parmesan.

Stuffed and baked Savoy cabbage

**Serves 4 as a starter
or side dish**

8 large Savoy cabbage leaves
400g (14oz) peeled butternut
  squash, cut into roughly
  2cm (¾in) pieces
600g (1lb 5oz) peeled Désirée
  or Cyprus potatoes, cut into
  roughly 2cm (¾in) pieces
4 tbsp extra-virgin olive oil
2 medium leeks, sliced into
  1cm (½in) rounds
1 garlic clove, finely sliced
250g (9oz) portobello
  mushrooms, sliced 1cm
  (½in) thick
100g (3½oz) vacuum-packed
  chestnuts, roughly chopped
1 tsp thyme leaves
250ml (9fl oz) double
  (heavy) cream
150g (5½oz) parmesan, grated
sea salt and freshly ground
  black pepper

**Savoy cabbages are great value for money and are
surprisingly robust. These stuffed cabbage leaves are full
of flavour and the creamy parmesan sauce is the perfect
accompaniment. When you cut the leaves off, do it carefully
with a small knife so you cut the stem and the leaf comes off
without tearing. Keep the leftover heads of the cabbage, as
they are delicious shredded, boiled, and tossed in butter and
black pepper.**

Blanch the cabbage leaves 2 at a time for 3 minutes in a pan
of boiling salted water, then transfer to a bowl of iced water to
cool them quickly. Add the squash to the boiling water and cook
for 5 minutes, then take out with a slotted spoon and drain on
kitchen paper. Add the potatoes to the same boiling water and
cook until they are just cooked but not too soft. Drain and keep
to one side.

Add 3 tablespoons of the olive oil to a hot, large non-stick frying
pan with the leeks, garlic, mushrooms, chestnuts and thyme.
Cook over a medium heat for 20 minutes so all the vegetables
become soft and sticky. Add the cooked potatoes and squash,
mix well and check the seasoning. Remove from the heat and
allow to cool, then divide into 8 equal portions.

Meanwhile, preheat the oven to 180°C/160°C fan/350°F/Gas 4.

Take a blanched cabbage leaf and lay it out flat on a chopping
board. Place a portion of filling at the stem end and tuck in the
sides of the leaf, so the filling is enclosed within the blanched
leaf, then roll it up. Repeat with the remaining cabbage leaves
and filling.

Rub the remaining 1 tablespoon of olive oil over the insides
of a baking dish, then place all 8 filled cabbage leaves in the
dish in a single layer. Pour over the cream, sprinkle over the
parmesan and bake in the oven for 20 minutes until golden
in places.

Serve on warm plates as a starter or as a side dish, with the
sauce from the baking dish spooned over.

Portobello mushroom and leek al forno

Serves 4

5 tbsp extra-virgin olive oil
1 tsp thyme leaves
1 garlic clove, crushed to
  a paste with a little sea salt
600g (1lb 5oz) portobello
  mushrooms, sliced 1cm
  (½in) thick
3 medium leeks, sliced into
  2cm (¾in) rounds
50g (1¾oz) breadcrumbs
50g (1¾oz) parmesan, grated
sea salt and freshly ground
  black pepper

For the béchamel
50g (1¾oz) butter
40g (1½oz) plain
  (all-purpose) flour
500ml (17fl oz) hot milk
100g (3½oz) parmesan, grated

It's always surprising how much water there is in a mushroom, and one of the reasons for using portobello mushrooms for this recipe is the fact that they hold their shape well and are not too watery. If you are using a regular flat-cap mushroom, increase the quantity of mushrooms by another 200g (7oz).

This is a really simple dish that doesn't require too much preparation and has lots of flavour.

Add 2 tablespoons of the olive oil to a hot, large non-stick frying pan, then add the thyme, crushed garlic in salt, mushrooms, and some salt and black pepper. Cook for 20 minutes over a medium heat, stirring occasionally. When the mushrooms are slightly sticky and the flavour is concentrated, remove the mushrooms from the pan and place in a bowl to one side.

Wipe the pan and add another 2 tablespoons of the olive oil. Add the leeks with some salt and black pepper and cook for 20 minutes, stirring occasionally, until soft. Take the leeks out of the pan and keep to one side. (The reason for cooking the leeks and mushrooms separately is that if they were cooked together the texture of the mushroom and leek would be a bit slimy and the flavours would not be as distinct.)

Preheat the oven to 180°C/160°C fan/350°F/Gas 4.

To make the béchamel, melt the butter in a medium saucepan, then add the flour and cook for 3 minutes, stirring with a wooden spoon. Slowly add the hot milk, stirring continuously to avoid any lumps. When you have added all the milk, cook over a low heat for 15 minutes. Finally, stir in the parmesan, remove from the heat and leave to one side.

Rub the insides of a baking dish with the remaining tablespoon of olive oil so the inside is completely covered, then add the cooked mushrooms so they sit at the bottom of the dish. Place the cooked leeks on top, then cover with the béchamel.

Mix the breadcrumbs and grated parmesan together and sprinkle on top, then bake in the oven for 25 minutes, until the top is a light golden brown and the sides of the dish are bubbling. Remove from the oven and rest for 5 minutes before serving; this will make it easier to spoon.

BROCCOLI

Broccoli and fontina croquettes

Makes 20

1kg (2lb 3oz) Désirée
   potatoes, peeled and cut into
   roughly 3cm (1¼in) pieces
150g (5½oz) fontina or
   Gruyère, grated
75g (2½oz) unsalted butter
1 egg, beaten
300g (10½oz) tenderstem
   broccoli, tough ends
   removed
500ml (17fl oz) sunflower oil
lemon wedges, for squeezing
sea salt and freshly ground
   black pepper

For the coating
200g (7oz) plain (all-purpose)
   flour, plus extra for dusting
2 eggs, beaten
200g (7oz) breadcrumbs

These little potato and broccoli croquettes are simple to make and perfect for a gathering with drinks. The smoother the mashed potato, the better they taste. Potato and broccoli work really well together and, with the addition of fontina, which has a distinctive flavour without being overpowering, make for a very tasty bite-sized potato snack.

Add the potatoes and a good pinch of salt to a large pan of water. Bring to the boil, then simmer for 20 minutes until the potatoes are fully cooked and soft. Drain into a colander and leave to cool for 5 minutes, then place back in the dry pan and add the grated cheese, butter and beaten egg. Using a large whisk, push down on the mixture and whisk so the potatoes turn into a mash. The more you do this, the smoother the mash becomes. Leave to one side.

Add the tenderstem broccoli to a medium saucepan of boiling salted water and cook for 4 minutes after the water has come back to the boil. Drain into a colander and leave to cool, then finely chop and whisk into the potato mixture, with salt and black pepper to taste. Divide the mixture into quarters and place each on the kitchen surface with a little flour to prevent them sticking. Roll each into a long, even sausage using the palm of your hands, then cut each sausage into 5 equal pieces. Place on a floured tray or plate and transfer to the fridge for 30 minutes.

Preheat the oven to 150°C/130°C fan/300°F/Gas 2.

Take 3 shallow bowls and place the flour in one, the beaten egg in another and the breadcrumbs in the third. With one hand, slowly and carefully roll each potato croquette in the flour, then the beaten egg and finally the breadcrumbs.

Once you have all the croquettes coated, place a medium, heavy-based saucepan over a high heat and add the sunflower oil. Heat until it reads 170°C/325°F on a cooking thermometer (or when a few breadcrumbs dropped into the oil turn golden in a few seconds), then turn the heat down to medium. Add 4 croquettes at a time to the hot oil and cook until lightly golden. Remove with a slotted spoon and place them on a wire rack with a tray underneath to catch any excess oil. Repeat until all the croquettes have been cooked, then place them all on an oven tray and transfer to the oven for a few minutes to ensure they are all hot. Sprinkle with some salt and serve as a canapé or as a snack, with lemons for squeezing.

Burrata and broccoli bruschetta

Serves 4 as a starter

500g (1lb 2oz) purple
  sprouting broccoli,
  tough ends removed
4 tbsp extra-virgin olive oil,
  plus extra for drizzling
1 garlic clove, thinly sliced
1 red chilli, deseeded and
  finely chopped
1 ciabatta loaf
150g (5½oz) burrata, finely
  chopped to a pulp
sea salt and freshly ground
  black pepper

**Purple sprouting broccoli is the most flavoursome of all
the broccolis; the purple heads turn green when you cook
it and it has sweet, tender leaves. The stem can be a bit
tough, so take your time in preparing the ends. I find splitting
them at the base helps them to cook evenly. In this recipe
the broccoli heads will break up, but that is not a bad thing,
as they become soft and squash nicely onto the bread.**

Add the purple sprouting broccoli to a large pan of boiling
salted water and cook for 5 minutes after the water has come
back to the boil. Drain into a colander.

Wipe the same pan dry and put back over a medium heat with
the olive oil, garlic and chilli. Cook for 1 minute, then add the
purple sprouting broccoli and some salt and black pepper to
taste, and cook slowly for 5 minutes. Don't worry if the broccoli
heads break up; this is good.

Cut 4 good slices of ciabatta and place in your toaster or under
a grill (broiler) until golden brown on both sides. Place on a large
plate then divide the purple sprouting broccoli mixture between
them. Finish off with the chopped burrata evenly placed on top
of the broccoli, and a drizzle of olive oil. Eat immediately.

Broccoli and potato frittata

Serves 4

500g (1lb 2oz) Désirée or
   Cyprus potatoes, peeled
   and cut into roughly 3cm
   (1¼in) pieces
300g (10½oz) tenderstem
   broccoli, tough ends
   removed
4 tbsp extra-virgin olive oil
1 medium onion, finely sliced
6 eggs
75ml (2¼fl oz) double
   (heavy) cream
100g (3½oz) parmesan, grated
8 basil leaves
sea salt and freshly ground
   black pepper

**I first made this frittata when I had very little left in the
fridge. The potato makes it more substantial, and the
addition of parmesan and cream ensures comfort. Either
eaten hot straight from the pan with a salad, or cut into
small pieces as a canapé and served cold, this is a delicious
frittata to whip up.**

Preheat the oven to 180°C/160°C fan/350°F/Gas 4.

Add the potatoes to a saucepan, fill with cold water and add
a good pinch of salt. Bring to the boil, then turn down the heat to
a simmer and cook for about 20 minutes. Check the potatoes are
cooked with the tip of a sharp knife; if there is no resistance then
it is cooked. Drain into a colander and let the steam evaporate.

Bring a saucepan of salted water to the boil, add the tenderstem
broccoli, bring back to the boil and cook for 3 minutes. Drain
into a colander and leave to cool. When cool, roughly chop and
keep to one side.

Add 2 tablespoons of the olive oil to a hot, large, non-stick,
ovenproof frying pan, add the onion and cook over a medium
heat for 10 minutes or until soft. Take the cooked onion out of
the pan and keep to one side. Clean the pan and place back
over a low heat.

In a large bowl, beat the eggs with a whisk until smooth and
combined, add the cream, the cooled broccoli, potatoes,
parmesan, cooked onion and some salt and black pepper.
Rip up the basil leaves, add to the bowl and give all the
ingredients a really good stir, so everything is combined.

Add the remaining 2 tablespoons of olive oil to the hot frying
pan, then add the frittata mixture. Leave the pan for a couple
of minutes then give it a wiggle, so you can see the eggs coming
away from the sides of the pan. Place the pan in the oven and
cook for 10 minutes. Check the frittata is cooked by giving it
another wiggle; if nothing moves then the frittata is ready.

Take out of the oven and leave to cool down for 10 minutes. Put
the pan back over the heat for a minute and place a plate on top,
then, holding the pan with a tea (dish) towel or oven glove, invert
the frittata onto the plate. Serve with a green salad.

Fritto of tenderstem broccoli with salsa rossa

Serves 4

500ml (17fl oz) sunflower oil
800g (1lb 12oz) tenderstem
  broccoli, tough ends
  trimmed
sea salt and freshly ground
  black pepper

For the batter
200g (7oz) tipo 00 flour
50ml (1¾fl oz) extra-virgin
  olive oil
1 egg white, beaten

For the salsa rossa
2 tbsp extra-virgin olive oil
2 red (bell) peppers,
  deseeded and each
  cut into 8 pieces
2 garlic cloves, halved
2 red chillies, halved
  and deseeded
150g (5½oz) datterini or
  cherry tomatoes, halved
400ml (14fl oz) tomato passata
  (strained tomatoes)
6 basil leaves

Tenderstem is widely available these days, so making this dish for a gathering of family or friends is hassle-free. Ensure you serve the fried tenderstem immediately so it is hot and crispy. You may need more than you think!

Preheat the oven to 180°C/160°C fan/350°F/Gas 4.

Make the salsa rossa. Rub the insides of a baking dish with the olive oil, add the red pepper, garlic, chillies, tomatoes and passata, then mix with a spoon to combine the ingredients. Season with salt and black pepper and cover the dish tightly with foil. Bake in the oven for 25 minutes, then take off the foil and bake for a further 5 minutes. Take the dish out of the oven and leave to cool. When cool, transfer to a food processor or blender with the basil and blitz until smooth. Check the seasoning and leave to one side.

To make the batter, add the flour to a large bowl with the olive oil and beaten egg white. Whisk in enough warm water to make the batter the same consistency as runny honey. If you add too much water and the batter seems to thin, add another tablespoon of flour. Cover and place in the fridge for 15 minutes.

Add the sunflower oil to a large frying pan and heat until it reads 180°C/356°F on a cooking thermometer (or test by adding a drop of batter to the oil – if it sizzles and turns golden within a few seconds, it is ready).

In batches, carefully dip each tenderstem in the batter so it is completely coated, then gently place in the hot oil. Cook for about 4 minutes, until the tenderstem goes golden brown. Remove with a slotted spoon and place on a wire rack with a tray underneath to catch any excess oil.

When you have cooked all the tenderstem, scatter them with a sprinkle of salt and pop them in the oven for 3 minutes, to ensure they are really hot.

Arrange the tenderstem fritto on a large platter and spoon the salsa rossa into a small bowl. Serve in the middle of the table for everyone to dip and enjoy.

Tenderstem broccoli purée with mezze maniche

Serves 4

300g (10½oz) tenderstem
  broccoli, tough ends
  removed
2 garlic cloves, peeled
75ml (2¼fl oz) new season
  olive oil (if available – or use
  what you have to hand)
400g (14oz) dried mezze
  maniche pasta
100g (3½oz) pecorino, grated
sea salt and freshly ground
  black pepper

New season olive oil is one of the highlights of the year. The dark green oil is something very special, and in Italy it is used in many dishes as soon as it is available. Mezze maniche pasta holds the sauce of tenderstem broccoli purée and peppery oil perfectly. You don't want to cook the sauce too much, as prolonged heat will diminish the flavour of the new oil, which is why you should stir in half the sauce as you serve it. Purists would probably not add pecorino, but I love adding a little bit.

Add the tenderstem broccoli and garlic to a pan of boiling salted water and cook for 10 minutes until soft. Use a slotted spoon to transfer the broccoli and garlic to a blender, keeping the cooking water in the pan. Add a cupful of the broccoli cooking water to the blender and purée until smooth and it easily coats the back of a spoon. Pour the purée into a bowl and, with a balloon whisk, slowly incorporate the olive oil, whisking so the sauce absorbs the oil. Add salt and black pepper to taste and leave to one side.

Bring the broccoli cooking water back to the boil, add the mezze maniche and cook for 3 minutes less than the packet suggests. Take out the pasta with a slotted spoon and place in a hot non-stick frying pan with 2 ladlefuls of the pasta cooking water. Cook for 1 minute, stirring with a wooden spoon, then add half the broccoli purée and cook over a medium heat, stirring so the pasta and sauce start to become emulsified and reduced.

Check the seasoning and place in warm pasta bowls with the remaining broccoli purée spooned on top of each portion. Serve with the grated pecorino and some black pepper.

Zuppa del povero

Serves 4

20g (¾oz) dried porcini
   mushrooms, soaked in
   2 litres (68fl oz) hot water
   for 15 minutes
3 tbsp extra-virgin olive oil,
   plus extra for drizzling
2 carrots, finely chopped
1 medium leek, finely sliced
1 tsp thyme leaves
1 garlic clove, sliced,
   plus 1 peeled clove for
   rubbing the ciabatta
2 celery stalks, finely sliced
300g (10½oz) trimmed purple
   sprouting broccoli heads,
   halved lengthways
1 tbsp chopped flat-leaf
   parsley
1 ciabatta loaf
75g (2½oz) parmesan, grated
sea salt and freshly ground
   black pepper

Cucina povera is a very important part of Italy's food heritage. It's all about frugal cooking using foraged ingredients to make food that is filling but satisfies the palate.

Purple sprouting broccoli is delicious and tender if you cut off the tough bottom stems. The ciabatta crostini with lots of parmesan pushed into it makes the soup even nicer – if you choose to pop the breads into the bowls before adding the soup they become really soft and comforting. This is a soup to serve on a cold winter's day. Add a drizzle of new season olive oil when serving to make it really special.

Remove the porcini from their soaking liquid, finely chop and set aside. Strain the soaking liquid through some kitchen paper or a paper coffee filter to remove any grit, then leave to one side.

Add the olive oil to a hot, large saucepan with the carrots, leek, thyme, sliced garlic and celery, and a good pinch of salt. Cook over a low heat for 15 minutes, then add the chopped porcini and cook for a further 5 minutes. Add the porcini soaking liquid, check the seasoning and bring to a simmer. Add the purple sprouting broccoli and cook for 10 minutes until tender, then add the parsley. The soup will appear to be more of a broth than a soup; it's no looker but tastes great.

Preheat the oven to 180°C/160°C fan/350°F/Gas 4.

Cut 4 generous slices of ciabatta, drizzle them with a little olive oil and sprinkle over a pinch of salt. Place in the oven for 5 minutes until crisp, rub with the peeled garlic clove, then push the parmesan firmly onto each toast. Divide the soup between bowls, ensuring each bowl has some purple sprouting broccoli, then top each with a cheese toast. Alternatively, you can place a cheese toast in the bottom of each bowl before spooning the soup on top. Serve immediately.

Broccoli, squash and lentil salad with walnut pesto

Serves 4 as a starter or side

150g (5½oz) dried Umbrian
  or Puy (French) lentils
500g (1lb 2oz) butternut
  squash, peeled
500g (1lb 2oz) tenderstem
  broccoli, tough ends
  removed
3 tbsp extra-virgin olive oil
1 tbsp white balsamic vinegar
100g (3½oz) wild rocket
  (arugula)
sea salt and freshly ground
  black pepper

For the walnut pesto
1 garlic clove, peeled
½ tsp sea salt
100g (3½oz) walnuts
4 tbsp milk
100g (3½oz) parmesan, grated
juice of ½ lemon
4 tbsp extra-virgin olive oil
50g (1¾oz) breadcrumbs
1 tbsp chopped flat-leaf
  parsley

Grilled tenderstem and butternut squash are a lovely combination and mixed with the walnut pesto make a really comforting winter starter. I love lentils in a salad, as they make the dish more substantial and add texture. White balsamic is good to use in this salad, as it is not as sweet as regular balsamic – the grape must has not been reduced enough to make it caramelize, so it has a fruitier flavour and is not as concentrated.

First, make the walnut pesto. Place the garlic and salt in a pestle and mortar and crush to a fine paste, then add the walnuts and pound until smooth. Add the milk and grind until the sauce has emulsified, then add the parmesan, lemon juice and olive oil. Mix so the sauce is smooth and well combined, then stir in the breadcrumbs and parsley so you have a thick-set sauce that looks a bit like hummus. Place to one side.

Add the lentils to a small saucepan and add water to come 5cm (2in) above the level of the lentils. Cook for 20 minutes or until the lentils are tender and have a little bite. Drain and put to one side.

Cut the peeled butternut squash in half lengthways and scoop out the seeds and stringy bits from the centre. Lay cut side down on a chopping board (this will make it easier to slice). With a sharp knife, cut 1cm (½in) slices from the top of the stem down to the base. Do the same with the other half. Don't worry if the slices aren't the same thickness – and some will be crescent-moon shape because of the scooped-out core – it's all about the flavour.

Add the squash slices to a large pan of boiling salted water and bring the water back to the boil. When the water is boiling again, remove the squash slices with a slotted spoon and carefully lay them flat on a tea (dish) towel to soak up any excess water. Discard the cooking water and fill up the saucepan again with water and a good pinch of salt.

When the water has come to the boil, add the tenderstem and bring the water back to the boil. When the water is boiling again, take out the tenderstem and lay on another tea towel to soak up any excess water, just as you did with the squash.

Continued overleaf

Broccoli, squash and lentil salad with walnut pesto
continued

When the tenderstem and butternut squash have cooled down and are dry, heat up a griddle pan so it is very hot. Take a few slices of the butternut squash and place them on the hot griddle pan. Don't touch them for 2 minutes and then, with a pair of tongs or a roasting fork, carefully turn them over. When both sides of the squash have grill marks on them, place on a wire rack to cool. This will stop them from getting soggy and wet. Repeat this until you have cooked all the squash.

Do the same with the tenderstem, so both ingredients are grilled. Cut the tenderstem in half lengthways and leave to one side.

To make the salad, add the olive oil, vinegar and some salt and black pepper to a large bowl and whisk so the dressing is smooth. Add the wild rocket and lentils, the grilled squash and tenderstem, and mix carefully. Divide the salad between 4 plates or arrange on a platter and drizzle over the walnut pesto. If there is any of the walnut pesto left, it will keep it in the fridge for 24 hours.

Yellow pepper, broccoli and squash salad with pine nuts

Serves 4 as a starter

150g (5½oz) dried Umbrian
    or Puy (French) lentils
1 medium butternut squash,
    peeled
6 tbsp extra-virgin olive oil
1 tsp thyme leaves
4 yellow (bell) peppers
400g (14oz) tenderstem
    broccoli, tough ends
    removed
1 small shallot, finely diced
2 tbsp red wine vinegar
2 tbsp honey
75g (2½oz) pine nuts, toasted
    to a light golden brown
sea salt and freshly ground
    black pepper

**As you can see, I do like to use tenderstem and squash
in a salad! This is a variation of the salad on the previous
page, with sharp and syrupy notes. Adding grilled peppers
makes this salad sweet and smoky, and the addition of
finely chopped shallot, red wine vinegar and honey balances
everything wonderfully. Whereas the salad on page 149 is
perfect for wintertime, I like to enjoy this version in late
summer or early autumn.**

Preheat the oven to 180°C/160°C fan/350°F/Gas 4.

Add the lentils to a small saucepan and add water to come
5cm (2in) above the level of the lentils. Cook for 20 minutes
or until the lentils are tender and still have a little bite. Drain
and put to one side.

Cut the peeled butternut squash in half lengthways and scoop
out the seeds and stringy bits from the centre. Lay the butternut
squash cut side down on a chopping board, cut in half lengthways
and then cut into 2cm (¾in) slices.

In a large bowl, mix the squash with 1 tablespoon of the olive oil,
the thyme and some salt and black pepper. Place on a roasting
tray and cover with foil, so there are no gaps. Put the tray in the
oven and cook for 25 minutes, then remove the foil and check
the squash is cooked with the tip of a sharp knife; if there is no
resistance, then it is cooked. Place the squash back in the oven
for a further 5 minutes (without the foil) to dry it out a little, then
remove from the oven and leave to one side to cool.

Cut the yellow peppers in half lengthways and place on a baking
tray, shiny side up. Put the tray in the oven, turn on the grill
(broiler) element, and cook until the peppers start to blister.
This will take about 15 minutes. When the peppers have a
charred skin, remove the tray from the oven, place the peppers
in a bowl and cover with cling film (plastic wrap). Leave the
peppers to cool, then remove the skin and any seeds. Cut the
peppers into strips 2cm (¾in) thick.

Add the broccoli to a pan of boiling salted water and cook for
2 minutes after the water has come back to the boil. Remove
from the pan and leave to one side to cool. When cool, pat dry
with some kitchen paper to absorb any excess water (if the
broccoli is too wet it will make the dressing watery).

Continued overleaf

Yellow pepper, broccoli and squash salad with pine nuts
continued

Add the shallot, vinegar and honey, with some salt and black pepper, to a large bowl. Using a balloon whisk, mix, then start adding the remaining 5 tablespoons of olive oil, a spoonful at a time, whisking so the dressing is emulsified.

Place the cooked tenderstem on a large serving plate, then scatter over the roasted squash, lentils and then the yellow pepper slices. Drizzle over the dressing evenly and finally scatter the toasted pine nuts on top. Serve in the middle of the table – as the salad is served, the dressing will mix in well with all the vegetables.

Creamy broccoli, leek and tomato pasta

Serves 4 as a starter

500g (1lb 2oz) calabrese
  broccoli, rough end removed
  and each broccoli cut into
  4 pieces
2 tbsp extra-virgin olive oil
2 medium leeks, sliced into
  2cm (¾in) rounds
1 garlic clove, finely sliced
1 mild red chilli, deseeded
  and finely chopped
150g (5½oz) datterini
  tomatoes, quartered
75ml (2¼fl oz) double
  (heavy) cream
500g (1lb 2oz) dried
  paccheri pasta
100g (3½oz) parmesan, grated
1 tbsp chopped flat-leaf
  parsley
sea salt and freshly ground
  black pepper

Calabrese broccoli has slightly gone out of fashion due to other varieties widely available – tenderstem, purple sprouting and rapini – but it is delicious. The stems are the sweetest part and should always be used, as they have so much flavour. Paccheri pasta works perfectly here, catching all the creamy sauce.

Add the broccoli pieces to a large pan of boiling salted water and cook until the water comes back to the boil. Remove the broccoli with a slotted spoon and keep to one side. Keep the water over a low heat (it will be used to cook the pasta).

Add the olive oil to a hot, large non-stick frying pan, add the leeks and a good pinch of salt and cook for 15 minutes, stirring occasionally. When soft and sticky, add the garlic, chilli, cooked broccoli and the tomato quarters. Cook for 5 minutes, then add the cream and cook for a further 5 minutes, adding a ladleful of the broccoli cooking water if the sauce seems a little dry.

Turn up the heat on the broccoli water and add some more boiling water from the kettle so the pan is over three-quarters full. Add the pasta, stirring it around for the first couple of minutes of cooking so it doesn't sink to the bottom of the pan and stick. Cook for 3 minutes less than the packet suggests, then remove the pasta with a slotted spoon and add to the broccoli pan. Add 2 ladlefuls of pasta cooking water and cook for a further 3 minutes, shaking the pan frequently so the pasta and the sauce start to emulsify and the broccoli breaks up a little. Add half the parmesan and the all the parsley, stir together, check the seasoning and finish off with some black pepper.

Serve at once in warm pasta bowls, with the remaining parmesan sprinkled on top of each bowl of pasta.

Lasagne of broccoli, potatoes and sweet onions

Serves 4

3 tbsp extra-virgin olive oil,
  plus extra for greasing
4 medium onions, thinly sliced
1 tsp thyme leaves
60g (2¼oz) butter
50g (1¾oz) plain
  (all-purpose) flour
700ml (24fl oz) hot milk
100g (3½oz) parmesan,
  grated, plus extra to finish
400g (14oz) Calabrese
  broccoli, rough end removed
  and each broccoli cut
  into 4 pieces
4 medium Désirée or Cyprus
  potatoes, peeled and cut into
  5mm (¼in) slices
300g (10½oz) dried egg
  lasagne sheets
sea salt and freshly ground
  black pepper

Lasagne is a great way to feed lots of people with very little hassle and mess at a mealtime, and is also filling and inexpensive to make. Make sure the béchamel is nicely seasoned and has a strong parmesan flavour. If the potatoes still seem a bit firm when layering, don't worry, they will cook through when you bake the lasagne. The sweet onions add richness and flavour, making this a real comfort food dish.

Add 2 tablespoons of the olive oil to a hot, large frying pan, then add the onions, thyme and a pinch of salt and cook over a low heat for 20 minutes, until the onions are soft and sweet. Keep to one side.

While the onions are cooking, melt the butter in a medium saucepan, add the flour and cook for 3 minutes, stirring with a wooden spoon. Slowly add the hot milk, stirring continuously to avoid any lumps. When you have added all the milk, cook over a low heat for 15 minutes, then add the parmesan, stir thoroughly, take off the heat and leave to one side.

Add the broccoli to a pan of boiling salted water and cook for 3 minutes after the water has come back to the boil. Take the broccoli pieces out with a slotted spoon and leave to cool down. Add the potato slices to the boiling water and cook for 3 minutes after the water has come back to the boil, then drain into a colander and leave to cool down.

Preheat the oven to 180°C/160°C fan/350°F/Gas 4.

Take a baking dish and rub the remaining tablespoon of olive oil all over the insides of the dish. Place a layer of the pasta sheets on the base of the dish, then spread over a quarter of the béchamel. Follow with a third of the potatoes, a third of the onions and then a third of the broccoli pieces, adding a grind of black pepper between each vegetable layer. Place another layer of pasta sheets on top and repeat until you have 3 layers. Finish with a final layer of pasta sheets and the remaining béchamel spread over the top. Sprinkle the lasagne with a little parmesan.

Cover with greased foil and cook in the oven for 35 minutes. Remove the foil and cook for a further 10 minutes, so the top of the lasagne gets a little colour and the edges crisp up. Leave to cool for 10 minutes before serving.

TOMATOES

Tagliatelle with tomatoes, zucchini and capers

Serves 4 as a starter

3 medium courgettes
(zucchini)
3 tbsp extra-virgin olive oil
1 garlic clove, finely sliced
1 red chilli, deseeded and
finely chopped
300g (10½oz) datterini
tomatoes, quartered
25g (1oz) capers in vinegar,
drained
250g (9oz) fresh tagliatelle
1 tbsp chopped flat-leaf
parsley
sea salt and freshly ground
black pepper

**Datterini tomatoes are something very special. They are
extremely sweet and have thin skins so are perfect for
a quick tomato sauce. It is important not to cook them
too much, as the flavour is best when they are just starting
to break up. The courgettes and capers are a lovely addition
to the tomatoes. As the sauce is so simple, it's important
to finish cooking the tagliatelle in the sauce, so the pasta
really absorbs the flavour.**

Slice the courgettes into 1cm (½in) rounds, stack 3 slices on
top of each other, then cut into 4 so you end up with 5mm (¼in)
matchsticks, repeating until you have cut all the courgettes.

Add the olive oil to a hot, large non-stick frying pan, then add
the garlic, red chilli, courgettes and a good pinch of salt. Cook
for 10 minutes over a medium heat, then add the quartered
tomatoes and the capers. Stir for a moment to heat through,
then take the pan off the heat and keep to one side.

Add the tagliatelle to a large pan of boiling salted water and cook
for 2 minutes, then remove from the water using a pair of tongs
and transfer to the pan with the courgettes and tomatoes. Place
the pan back over a medium heat and add 2 ladlefuls of the
pasta cooking water and the parsley. Stir with a wooden spoon
and reduce the liquid so the pasta and the sauce cook together,
and the sauce becomes emulsified. Add black pepper and check
if it needs more salt. Serve immediately in warm pasta bowls.

Pappa al pomodoro

Serves 8

4 tbsp extra-virgin olive oil,
plus extra to serve
2 garlic cloves, finely sliced
1kg (2lb 3oz) ripe plum
tomatoes, top bit cut out,
quartered
8 basil leaves, torn
600ml (20fl oz) tomato passata
(strained tomatoes)
600ml (20fl oz) boiling water
2 stale ciabatta loaves, crusts
removed, torn by hand into
4cm (1½in) chunks
sea salt and freshly ground
black pepper

Many years ago, while working at The River Café, Ruthie Rogers was showing me the art of making pappa al pomodoro. (Ruthie is the best soup maker and I was lucky enough to learn from her – she can make a soup out of a handful of ingredients and it always tastes amazing. Just as with this recipe, most of her soups then had bread in them – the trick was to cook the bread until it became almost invisible.) On this particular occasion we had the late, great Antonio Carluccio in for lunch and he ordered the pappa al pomodoro that we had lovingly made with the finest jarred plum tomatoes. Ruthie and I went to say hello and asked him, did he like the pappa al pomodoro? He said it was delicious, but asked why we used jarred tomatoes when we could be using fresh? He was right, the tomato season was in full swing as it was early summer. We made it all summer with fresh tomatoes... Thank you Antonio, and thank you Ruthie, for teaching me the finer art of making pappa al pomodoro.

Add the olive oil to a large saucepan over a high heat, then add the garlic, tomatoes and half the basil and cook for 10 minutes, stirring occasionally. Add the passata, turn down the heat to low and cook for 25 minutes. The sauce should have reduced by half. Add a good pinch of salt and, using a stick blender, blitz the sauce so it is smooth and the tomato skins have been blended into the sauce.

Add the boiling water, bring the tomato sauce to a simmer, then stir in the ciabatta and cook for a further 12 minutes over a low heat so the bread starts to cook into the sauce and it becomes a very thick soup, almost resembling a bread sauce.

Add the remaining basil, check the seasoning, and finish off each serving with a generous drizzle of olive oil and some black pepper.

Pasta alla Sorrentina

Serves 4

4 tbsp extra-virgin olive oil
1 garlic clove, finely sliced
6 basil leaves, torn
600ml (20fl oz) tomato passata
(strained tomatoes)
500g (1lb 2oz) dried
paccheri pasta
250g (9oz) smoked scamorza,
grated on the coarsest part
of a box grater, plus extra
to serve
sea salt and freshly ground
black pepper

**I love this pasta dish; it has so much flavour, using only
a few ingredients. Paccheri pasta is essential, as its texture
and shape hold the sauce perfectly while the inside of the
tubes absorb the tomato flavour. I have used tomato passata
here but the dish can also be made with fresh tomatoes –
I would use 250g (9oz) datterini or cherry tomatoes cut in
half instead. Any leftovers can also be made into a pasta al
forno, but it's unlikely there will be any leftovers!**

Add the olive oil to a hot, large non-stick frying pan, then add
the garlic and half the basil leaves and cook for 1 minute. Pour
in the passata and bring to a simmer, then reduce the heat to
low. Leave to gently simmer for 15 minutes or until the passata
has reduced by half. Keep to one side.

Add the paccheri to a large pan of boiling salted water and stir
for the first 2 minutes to ensure it doesn't stick to the bottom of
the pan. Cook for 3 minutes less than the packet suggests, then
take out the al dente paccheri using a slotted spoon and place
in the frying pan with the tomato sauce and 2 ladlefuls of pasta
cooking water. Place the pan back over a medium heat, stirring
gently with a wooden spoon for 3 minutes. The pasta will absorb
the extra liquid and the sauce should be thickened from the
starch of the pasta.

Add the grated smoked scamorza and the remaining basil. Using
a wooden spoon, stir to make sure the pasta and scamorza are
well combined and the cheese has melted. It may look a little
'bitty' but it's all about the flavour. Check the seasoning and
serve immediately in warm pasta bowls with some extra smoked
scamorza on top of each portion.

Roasted stuffed tomatoes

Serves 4

8 large beef tomatoes
8 tbsp extra-virgin olive oil
2 medium onions, finely
    chopped
800g (14oz) chestnut (cremini)
    mushrooms, finely sliced
2 garlic cloves, finely sliced
2 tsp thyme leaves
300g (10½oz) Carnaroli
    risotto rice
1 litre (34fl oz) water
200g (7oz) parmesan, grated
8 slices of smoked scamorza
sea salt and freshly ground
    black pepper

A roasted stuffed tomato is a simple and delicious way to use large beef tomatoes, which tend to be a bit watery and are not always that flavoursome. The rice is cooked like a risotto so has maximum flavour and a creamy texture, and with the smoked scamorza on top, this easy dish tastes like more than the sum of its parts. Try to use ripe tomatoes as they will cook more evenly and the end result will be much better.

Preheat the oven to 180°C/160°C fan/350°F/Gas 4.

Cut the tops off the tomatoes so they have a lid. Scoop out and reserve the inside pulp so you are left with a tomato shell and lid. Keep to one side.

Add 6 tablespoons of the olive oil to a large frying pan over a medium heat, then add the onions, mushrooms, garlic, thyme, reserved tomato pulp and a good pinch of salt. Cook for 20 minutes so all the liquid from the mushrooms releases and reduces, along with the tomato mixture, to a sticky mixture. Remove from the heat and keep to one side.

Add the remaining 2 tablespoons of olive oil to a medium saucepan over a medium heat, add the rice, then add the water, stirring so the rice, oil and water are combined well; this will stop the rice from sticking to the sides of the pan. Place a lid on the pan, bring to the boil, then turn down the heat so the rice cooks slowly for 15 minutes. After 15 minutes there will be no liquid left, just al dente rice. Add the cooked mushroom and tomato mixture to the hot rice and cook together for 5 minutes, adding a few tablespoons of water if the mixture feels dry. Take off the heat and stir in the parmesan. Check the seasoning and add some black pepper.

Place the tomato shells snugly in an oven tray. With a tablespoon, carefully fill the shells with the rice mixture, then place a slice of smoked scamorza on each. Place the tomato lids on top, transfer to the oven and cook for 25 minutes, until the tomato is cooked and the rice mixture is bubbling inside the tomato. Leave to cool for 5 minutes before serving.

Tomato and goat's cheese salad with fried zucchini

Serves 4

4 medium courgettes
(zucchini)
350ml (12fl oz) sunflower oil
2 thin slices of sourdough
bread
1 garlic clove, crushed to
a paste with a little sea salt
2 tbsp red wine vinegar
1 red chilli, deseeded and
finely chopped
2 tbsp chopped mint leaves
8 best-quality ripe medium
tomatoes, sliced
8 basil leaves, torn
150g (5½oz) datterini
tomatoes, halved lengthways
125g (4½oz) soft goat's
cheese
sea salt and freshly ground
black pepper

A tomato salad in summer is a must, and adding some fried courgettes and salty goat's cheese makes the humble tomato salad into something really special. The more care you take in frying the courgettes, the better the salad will be. It is best assembled last minute with the courgettes cooked beforehand, so the tomatoes don't make everything else soggy.

Soft goat's cheese is much nicer here than the sort with a rind, as the flavour is less pronounced and it has a smooth, soft texture. Salted ricotta or feta will also work well.

On a mandoline or in a food processor, slice the courgettes into very thin rounds, then add a good sprinkling of salt and place them in a colander for 15 minutes. The courgettes will release lots of water. Rinse off the salt, then lay the sliced courgettes flat on a large, clean tea (dish) towel. Roll up the tea towel and push down with all your weight so the water from the courgettes gets absorbed by the tea towel.

Add the sunflower oil to a hot, large non-stick frying pan and fry the courgettes in 4 batches, until golden brown, placing each cooked batch on a wire rack. When the courgettes are cool, place on top of some kitchen paper to absorb excess oil (do not put kitchen paper on top of them or the crisp courgette slices will break). Leave to one side.

Tear the sourdough slices into small pieces and fry until golden brown in the sunflower oil you cooked the courgettes in. Remove, sprinkle with salt and keep to one side.

To make the dressing, add the crushed garlic in salt to a large bowl with the vinegar, chilli and mint. Mix well, then add the fried courgettes and gently toss so the crisp courgettes absorb the dressing.

Lay the slices of tomato carefully on a large serving plate with the torn basil leaves on top, then add the halved datterini tomatoes so they are evenly distributed. Add the goat's cheese all over in small pieces, grind some black pepper on top and then place the dressed courgettes on top, with the fried sourdough toasts scattered all over. Serve in the middle of the table as a starter to share.

Puff pastry pizza

Serves 4

3 tbsp extra-virgin olive oil
1 garlic clove, sliced
12 taggiasche or niçoise
   olives, pitted and
   roughly chopped
25g (1oz) miniature capers
   in vinegar, drained
200g (7oz) cherry tomatoes,
   quartered
1 tbsp chopped fresh oregano
600ml (20fl oz) tomato passata
   (strained tomatoes)
1 x 320g (11¼oz) sheet
   of ready-rolled all-butter
   puff pastry
flour, for dusting
1 egg, beaten, for egg wash
250g (9oz) ricotta
75g (2½oz) parmesan, grated
sea salt

Shop-bought puff pastry is very convenient and is always very consistent; the best ones are made from 100% butter. This recipe has a similarity to a pizza but with the crispness of puff pastry – egg wash gives the pastry colour and flavour, so don't skip it. The tomato sauce here is strong in taste with the addition of olives, capers and oregano – one of my favourite combinations.

Add the olive oil to a hot, large non-stick frying pan and add the garlic, olives, capers, cherry tomatoes and oregano. Cook over a medium heat for 5 minutes, then add the passata with a good pinch of salt and cook over a low heat for 20 minutes, until the sauce has reduced by half and is thick. Keep to one side.

Meanwhile, preheat the oven to 180°C/160°C fan/350°F/Gas 4.

Place the sheet of puff pastry on a flat oven tray you have dusted with a little flour. Brush the egg wash all over the top of the pastry and cook in the oven for 15 minutes until golden brown and risen. Remove from the oven and leave to cool. When cool, carefully spoon on the tomato sauce, gently pushing down so the sauce sits nicely on the cooked pastry. Finish off with an even scattering of ricotta and grated parmesan on top.

Place back in the oven for 10 minutes, then serve as a lunch dish with a green salad, or cut into small pieces as a canapé.

Baked Sicilian rice

Serves 4

5 tbsp extra-virgin olive oil

2 medium spring onions (scallions) or 1 large white onion, finely chopped

1 garlic clove, finely chopped

3 celery stalks, finely chopped

2 medium carrots, finely chopped

250g (9oz) chestnut (cremini) mushrooms, finely sliced

600ml (20fl oz) tomato passata (strained tomatoes)

400g (14oz) basmati rice

2 tbsp chopped flat-leaf parsley

75g (2½oz) breadcrumbs

100g (3½oz) parmesan, grated

1 tsp thyme leaves

sea salt and freshly ground black pepper

I make this dish when there is very little in the fridge. It's easy to make and has loads of flavour, and a lovely crispy texture because of the breadcrumb topping. I serve it with some garlicky greens or broccoli on the side.

Preheat the oven to 180°C/160°C fan/350°F/Gas 4.

Add 3 tablespoons of the olive oil to a hot, large non-stick frying pan and add the spring onions, garlic, celery, carrots and chestnut mushrooms, with a good pinch of salt. Cook for 15 minutes over a low heat, stirring occasionally. Add the passata and cook for 10 minutes, still over a low heat. Season with plenty of black pepper and salt.

Add another tablespoon of olive oil to a saucepan over a medium heat, add the rice and stir so the rice and oil are mixed. Add water to come 3cm (1¼in) above the level of the rice, place a tight-fitting lid on top and cook over a medium heat for 5 minutes or until the water starts to boil, then turn down to a low heat for a further 5 minutes; this will steam the rice. Take off the heat and leave the rice, with the lid still on, for a further 5 minutes.

Tip the cooked rice into a large bowl and fluff it up using a fork. Add the cooked tomato and mushroom mixture with the parsley, mix well together and check the seasoning.

Rub the remaining 1 tablespoon of oil over the base of a baking dish, then spoon in the rice mixture so it is evenly spread and flat on top. In a medium bowl, mix together the breadcrumbs, parmesan and thyme and sprinkle this evenly on top of the rice.

Bake in the oven for 20 minutes. The top should be lightly golden and crispy; if not, put the grill (broiler) on for a couple of minutes to finish it off. Leave to cool for 10 minutes before serving.

Tomato and red pepper risotto with chopped burrata

Serves 4

3 red (bell) peppers
3 tbsp extra-virgin olive oil
2 celery stalks, finely diced
1 small onion, finely diced
400g (14oz) Carnaroli
  risotto rice
75ml (2¼fl oz) white wine
1.5 litres (50fl oz) hot
  vegetable stock (see
  page 19 for homemade)
300ml (10fl oz) tomato passata
  (strained tomatoes)
75g (2½oz) unsalted butter
100g (3½oz) parmesan, grated
6 basil leaves, torn
150g (5½oz) burrata,
  finely chopped
sea salt and freshly ground
  black pepper

Tomato risotto is a favourite of mine, especially with the addition of smoky grilled red peppers. It's important to chop them finely so they cook into the risotto and emulsify with the butter and parmesan. The burrata on top adds a decadent, extra-creamy finish to the cooked risotto.

Preheat the grill (broiler).

Place the red peppers on a baking tray lined with foil and place under the hot grill. Leave for 10 minutes, then turn over and cook for a further 10 minutes; the skins should be burnt on the outside. Place in a bowl and cover the bowl with cling film (plastic wrap), so the peppers steam in the bowl. After 15 minutes, remove the peppers from the bowl and peel off the blackened skin. Tear each pepper in half and, using a serrated knife, scrape off the seeds. Place the flesh on a chopping board and finely chop. Keep to one side.

Add the olive oil to a hot, large, straight-sided saucepan, and add the celery and onion. Cook for 3 minutes, then add the rice and cook for a further 3 minutes so the rice absorbs the oil and goes translucent. Add the wine and cook until it is absorbed, then start adding the hot vegetable stock, a ladleful at a time, so the rice is always just covered. Keep doing this for 10 minutes over a medium heat so the rice is bubbling away.

Add the passata and the chopped peppers and cook for 5 minutes, stirring continuously. Add another ladleful of stock and check the seasoning. The risotto should be wet at this point, almost soupy, and the rice should have a good bite. Keep stirring and start reducing the liquid so the risotto starts to thicken. Give the pan a good shake and, when you feel the risotto is becoming emulsified, add the butter, parmesan and basil.

Stir vigorously so all the ingredients are combined, then take the pan off the heat, place a lid on top and leave the risotto to stand for 2–3 minutes; this will help the risotto rice puff up and absorb more of the liquid. Take the lid off, check the seasoning and add some black pepper. Give the risotto one last vigorous stir and serve in warm pasta bowls with the chopped burrata on top.

Conchiglioni al forno with salsa pizzaiola and mozzarella

Serves 4

4 tbsp extra-virgin olive oil,
 plus extra to serve
1 garlic clove, finely sliced
10 taggiasche olives, pitted
 and roughly chopped
1 tsp oregano leaves,
 chopped
600ml (20fl oz) tomato passata
 (strained tomatoes)
500g (1lb 2oz) dried
 conchiglioni pasta
150g (5½oz) mozzarella,
 roughly cut into pieces
sea salt and freshly ground
 black pepper
parmesan, grated, to serve

Baked pasta dishes are great if you don't want the hassle of serving people last minute, as you can prep them ahead and then pop them in the oven when needed. The combination of tomato, olives, oregano and mozzarella here is a match made in heaven. Conchiglioni, or pasta shells, are perfect for baked pasta because they hold the sauce on the inside and outside – ensuring every mouthful tastes delicious.

Add 3 tablespoons of the olive oil to a hot, large non-stick frying pan, add the garlic, olives and oregano and cook for 1 minute. Add the passata and cook slowly over a medium-low heat for 15 minutes so the sauce has reduced by half. Season and keep to one side.

Preheat the oven to 180°C/160°C fan/350°F/Gas 4.

Cook the conchiglioni in a large pan of boiling salted water for 3 minutes less than the packet suggests. Take the pasta out of the water with a slotted spoon and add to the tomato sauce in the frying pan, along with 2 ladlefuls of pasta water. Put back over a low heat and cook for 2–3 minutes so the sauce and the pasta are emulsified, then check the seasoning.

Rub the remaining tablespoon of olive oil on the insides of a medium baking dish. Carefully tip in the cooked pasta and make sure it is evenly spread out in the dish. Scatter over the mozzarella and bake in the oven for 20 minutes.

Serve with some grated parmesan and extra olive oil on top.

Tomato and potato al forno

Serves 4

4 tbsp extra-virgin olive oil

2 red onions, finely sliced

12 taggiasche olives, pitted
and roughly chopped

25g (1oz) capers in vinegar,
drained

1 tsp thyme leaves

600ml (20fl oz) tomato passata
(strained tomatoes)

400g (14oz) plum tomatoes,
finely chopped

8 basil leaves, torn

1 garlic clove, crushed to
a paste with a little sea salt

1kg (2lb 3oz) Cyprus or
Désirée potatoes, peeled
and finely sliced on a
mandoline

150ml (5fl oz) double
(heavy) cream

75g (2½oz) breadcrumbs

1 tbsp chopped flat-leaf
parsley

75g (2½oz) parmesan, grated

sea salt and freshly ground
black pepper

**Tomatoes, potatoes and basil baked together turn into
something magical. The parmesan and breadcrumb topping
gives this dish a lovely texture which, combined with the
creamy and flavour-packed tomato sauce, makes for a very
comforting supper.**

Add 3 tablespoons of the olive oil to a hot, large non-stick frying
pan, add the onions, olives, capers and thyme and cook for
10 minutes over a medium heat. Add the passata and cook for
a further 10 minutes, until the sauce has reduced by half, then
add the chopped tomatoes, season with salt and black pepper
and stir through the basil. Keep to one side.

Preheat the oven to 180°C/160°C fan/350°F/Gas 4.

Rub the remaining 1 tablespoon of oil and the crushed garlic
in salt over the insides of a baking dish, so all the insides are
coated. Add half the tomato mixture to the base of the dish, then
carefully add a layer of sliced potatoes on top. Add the remaining
tomato mixture and finish with the remaining sliced potatoes on
top, so you have 2 layers.

Season the top with salt and black pepper, then pour over the
cream so the top layer of potatoes is covered. Tightly cover with
baking paper, then with foil, and bake in the oven for 50 minutes.
Put a knife through the foil; if the knife goes through the potatoes
with no resistance, take the dish out and remove the foil.

In a small bowl, mix the breadcrumbs, parsley and parmesan
together and carefully add to the top of the potatoes so the
mixture is evenly spread. Place back in the oven for 10 minutes
so the breadcrumbs go a light golden brown. Leave to stand for
10 minutes before you serve.

BEANS

Green beans with grilled polenta and parmesan

Serves 4

800g (1lb 12oz) fine green
  beans, topped and tailed
4 tbsp extra-virgin olive oil
2 garlic cloves, finely sliced
1 red chilli, deseeded and
  finely chopped
600ml (20fl oz) tomato passata
  (strained tomatoes)
8 basil leaves, torn
150g (5½oz) parmesan
  shavings
sea salt and freshly ground
  black pepper

For the polenta
400ml (14fl oz) water
100g (3½oz) Bramata polenta
  (coarse cornmeal)
50g (1¾oz) unsalted butter

I really don't like undercooked green beans – for me they taste best when collapsed a little. Added to a tomato sauce their flavour really shines. Buttered grilled polenta is a favourite of mine and works perfectly with these tomatoey green beans. Shaved parmesan on top is a must.

Preheat the oven to 150°C/130°C fan/300°F/Gas 2.

To make the set polenta, bring the water to a boil in a saucepan, add a pinch of salt and, when simmering, add the polenta gradually and use a balloon whisk to stir it in; it's important you add it gradually, so the polenta can be dispersed evenly and will therefore cook properly. Once you have added all the polenta, turn down the heat and cook gently for 30 minutes, until the polenta is starting to come away from the edges of the pan. Pour into a straight-sided ceramic dish so the polenta is 2cm (¾in) thick. Leave to cool and set firm.

When set, cut the polenta into 8 even strips. Heat a griddle pan until very hot, then add the polenta slices. Leave for 4 minutes, without touching them, so that the polenta forms a crust (this will make it easier to flip and will also add flavour). Carefully turn over each slice and cook for 4 minutes on the other side. Take off the heat and place on an oven tray. Rub the butter on one side of each piece of grilled polenta and place in the oven to keep warm.

Add the green beans in 2 batches to a large saucepan of boiling salted water and cook for 5 minutes after the water has come back to the boil. Take each batch out with a slotted spoon and place in a colander, then empty the pan and give it a good wipe.

Place the pan back over the heat with the olive oil, garlic and chilli. Cook for 1 minute, then add the passata and cook for 15 minutes until the passata has reduced by half. Add some salt and black pepper, then add the blanched green beans and cook over a low heat for 10 minutes, stirring occasionally, so the green beans and tomato combine. Add the basil and check the seasoning.

Place the warm polenta slices on a platter and arrange the tomatoey beans on top. Finish with a generous amount of parmesan shavings.

Cauliflower, carrot and borlotti bean soup

Serves 4

1 large cauliflower
1kg (2lb 3oz) carrots, peeled
4 tbsp extra-virgin olive oil,
  plus extra to serve
1 tsp thyme leaves
6 garlic cloves, peeled
4 celery stalks, finely chopped
2 medium leeks, sliced into
  1cm (½in) rounds
2 litres (68fl oz) boiling water
2 x 400g (14oz) cans of
  borlotti beans, rinsed
  and drained
200ml (7fl oz) crème fraîche,
  plus extra to serve
1 tbsp chopped flat-leaf
  parsley
sea salt and freshly ground
  black pepper

Cauliflower has become a very fashionable vegetable but hasn't increased in price that much, so it remains a very economical ingredient. Roasting cauliflower and carrots intensifies their flavour because of the natural sugars in them. They add lots of flavour to the soup and, when puréed with crème fraîche, make for a quick and easy warming meal.

Preheat the oven to 180°C/160°C fan/350°F/Gas 4.

Cut off the cauliflower florets and then cut them into even-sized pieces. Chop the stem into similar sized pieces. Cut the carrots in half lengthways and in half again. Place the cauliflower and carrots in a large bowl and add 2 tablespoons of the olive oil, the thyme, garlic cloves, and some salt and black pepper, and mix well so the oil and thyme coat the vegetables.

Transfer everything to a roasting dish lined with baking paper and cover tightly with foil. Bake in the oven for 45 minutes, then remove the foil and place the dish back in the oven for a further 10 minutes so the carrots and cauliflower can get a little colour. Take out of the oven and leave to one side.

While the carrots and cauliflower are cooking, place a large, heavy-based saucepan over a medium heat and add the remaining 2 tablespoons of olive oil, the celery, leeks, and a good pinch of salt. Cook gently for 25 minutes, so the vegetables become soft and sticky. Add the boiling water, bring to a simmer, then add the roasted carrots, cauliflower and garlic, along with the drained borlotti beans.

Cook for a further 20 minutes, then add the crème fraîche and parsley, and check the seasoning. Using a stick blender or food processor, blitz the soup until really smooth and creamy. Serve in warm bowls with an extra dollop of crème fraîche and a slick of olive oil on top, and some fresh bread for dipping.

Pasta e fagioli with fresh stracci

Serves 4

5 tbsp extra-virgin olive oil,
  plus extra to serve
1 garlic clove, finely sliced
600ml (20fl oz) tomato passata
  (strained tomatoes)
2 x 400g (14oz) cans of
  borlotti beans, drained
  and rinsed
2 tbsp chopped flat-leaf
  parsley
sea salt and freshly ground
  black pepper
parmesan, grated, to serve

For the pasta dough
350g (12oz) tipo 00 flour
25g (1oz) fine semolina flour,
  plus 50g (1¾oz) for dusting
2 whole eggs plus 4 egg
  yolks, beaten together
2 tbsp water

Pasta e fagioli sounds really heavy but it is not. The combination of the fresh pasta sheets with the sweet borlotti beans is filling but light. I love making this dish in the summer when fresh borlotti beans are in season, and I tend to use fresh tomatoes instead of passata, but either way this is a pasta dish you have to try. Stracci means 'rags' in Italian, so don't worry if the pasta shapes are not perfectly even.

Make the pasta dough. Combine both flours in a large bowl, then add the beaten eggs and water. Mix with a fork to combine, then use your hands to form a dough. Once smooth, wrap the dough in cling film (plastic wrap) and rest in the fridge for 20 minutes.

Divide the pasta dough into quarters. Take one piece and, using a rolling pin, roll until the pasta dough is thin enough to go through the rollers on your pasta machine. Place one end in the machine on the widest setting and roll it through. Fold the pasta in half and roll again. Repeat 4 times for each quarter of pasta. This process makes the pasta more elastic and durable.

Now you can start making the stracci pasta. Using semolina flour to dust, roll each quarter of dough through the machine, one at a time, until it is thin enough that you can see the silhouette of your hand behind it. Halve each pasta sheet and stack on a chopping board with a very good dusting of semolina flour between each.

Cut the pasta sheets in half lengthways, then cut each length into right-angled triangles. Place the pieces on a tray lined with baking paper and dusted with plenty of fine semolina flour, so they don't stick together. Leave to dry, uncovered, for at least 1 hour.

To make the sauce, heat a large frying pan over a medium heat and add 3 tablespoons of the olive oil and the garlic. Cook for 1 minute, then add the passata and cook slowly for 15 minutes, to reduce by half. Add the borlotti beans, parsley, and some salt and pepper, then leave over a low heat while you cook the pasta.

Add the stracci pasta to a large pan of boiling salted water and cook for 2 minutes, then, using a slotted spoon, transfer them to the tomato and borlotti bean sauce. Turn up the heat and add 2 ladlefuls of pasta cooking water and the remaining 2 tablespoons of olive oil. Stir well with a wooden spoon, moving the pan from side to side, until the sauce starts to emulsify.

When everything is combined and the sauce clings to the pasta, check the seasoning and add black pepper. Serve immediately in warm bowls with some parmesan and extra olive oil on top.

Tomatoey cannellini beans with aubergines and peppers

Serves 4

5 tbsp extra-virgin olive oil,
  plus extra to serve
2 medium aubergines
  (eggplants), cut into roughly
  2cm (¾in) pieces
2 red onions, finely sliced
2 yellow (bell) peppers,
  deseeded and cut into
  1cm (½in) strips
600ml (20fl oz) tomato passata
  (strained tomatoes)
3 x 400g (14oz) cans of
  cannellini beans, drained
  and rinsed
8 basil leaves, torn
sea salt and freshly ground
  black pepper

Canned cannellini beans are very easy to use and take the hassle out of having to soak and cook the dried variety. Always rinse off the liquid, as it can be a little starchy. This is a quick and flavoursome dish that requires little preparation but has loads of flavour.

Preheat the oven to 180°C/160°C fan/350°F/Gas 4.

Add 3 tablespoons of the olive oil to a large bowl, then add the aubergine pieces with some salt and black pepper. With your hand, mix the aubergines so they are coated in the olive oil, then spread them out on a baking tray lined with baking paper. Cook in the oven for 20 minutes, until lightly golden, then leave to one side.

Add the remaining 2 tablespoons of olive oil to a large saucepan and add the onions, yellow peppers and a good pinch of salt. Cook for 20 minutes over a low heat so they become sweet and sticky. Add the passata and cook for a further 10 minutes over a low heat, then add the cannellini beans and cook slowly for a further 10 minutes.

Add the cooked aubergines and the basil, then gently stir together, so the aubergines are mixed in well. Check the seasoning, then serve on a large plate in the middle of the table with a drizzle more olive oil on top. I like to serve some toasted bread rubbed with garlic and olive oil on the side for scooping.

Swiss chard and cannellini bean bake

Serves 4

1kg (2lb 3oz) Swiss chard,
 with stems
3 tbsp extra-virgin olive oil
1 garlic clove, finely sliced
1 red chilli, deseeded and
 finely chopped
1 medium leek, sliced into
 1cm (½in) rounds
3 x 400g (14oz) cans of
 cannellini beans, drained
 and rinsed
200ml (7fl oz) double
 (heavy) cream
75g (2½oz) dried
 breadcrumbs
1 tsp thyme leaves
100g (3½oz) parmesan, grated
sea salt and freshly ground
 black pepper

Swiss chard is a very versatile vegetable and comes in different colours and sizes; the French variety called 'blette' is probably the most common to find. The stems are thick and wide, with an unmistakable earthy taste. This is a frugal recipe – there is virtually no wastage, as all the Swiss chard stalk is used.

Separate the Swiss chard stems and leaves. Cut the stems into 1cm (½in) slices and the leaves into roughly 3cm (1¼in) pieces. Wash the Swiss chard thoroughly.

Add the chard stems to a saucepan of boiling salted water and cook for 4 minutes after the water comes back to the boil. Remove the stems with a slotted spoon and place in a colander. Add the chard leaves to the boiling water and cook for 2 minutes after the water has come back to the boil, then remove with a slotted spoon and place in the colander.

Preheat the oven to 180°C/160°C fan/350°F/Gas 4.

Add 2 tablespoons of the olive oil to a large non-stick frying pan, add the garlic and chilli and cook for 1 minute, then add the leek and a good pinch of salt. Cook for 10 minutes, until the leek becomes softer and collapses a little. Add the cannellini beans, chard stems and leaves and cook for 5 minutes so all the ingredients are combined. Add the cream and bring to the boil. Season to taste with salt and black pepper and take off the heat.

Rub the insides of a baking dish with the remaining tablespoon of olive oil, then spoon the cannellini bean and chard mixture into the dish, so the mixture is lying flat.

In a medium bowl, mix the breadcrumbs, thyme and parmesan together, then sprinkle this evenly on top of the bean and chard mixture. Bake in the oven for 20 minutes, so the breadcrumbs and parmesan turn a golden brown, then take out of the oven and leave to stand for 5 minutes before serving.

Summer minestrone

Serves 8

2 tbsp extra-virgin olive oil
3 celery stalks, finely chopped
2 carrots, finely chopped
2 medium leeks, chopped
1 tsp thyme leaves
10g (⅓oz) dried porcini
   mushrooms, broken into
   small pieces
2 medium Cyprus potatoes,
   or any waxy potato, cut into
   2cm (¾in) pieces
500g (1lb 2oz) medium
   courgettes (zucchini), cut in
   half lengthways then sliced
   into 1cm (½in) half-moons
300g (10½oz) fine green
   beans, topped and tailed and
   cut into 2cm (¾in) pieces
100g (3½oz) dried macaroni
2 x 400g (14oz) cans of
   borlotti beans, drained
   and rinsed
sea salt and freshly ground
   black pepper

For the pesto
½ garlic clove
100g (3½oz) basil leaves
75g (2½oz) pine nuts
   (untoasted)
75g (2½oz) parmesan,
   finely grated
2 tbsp water
150ml (5fl oz) extra-virgin
   olive oil

Summer brings with it an array of lovely vegetables and herbs. Courgettes are in abundance throughout summer, so should be used in many ways. This minestrone is a hearty soup without being too heavy – the addition of macaroni, borlotti beans, potatoes and pesto makes it wholesome and filling. There will always be some pesto left over, which makes a simple impromptu pasta dish the next day.

To make the soup base, add the olive oil to a hot, large saucepan, add the celery, carrots, leeks, thyme, porcini, potatoes and a good pinch of salt. Cover with a lid and cook over a medium heat for 20 minutes, stirring occasionally so all the ingredients cook evenly.

Meanwhile, cook the courgettes in a large pan of boiling salted water for 4 minutes after the water has come back to the boil. Remove with a slotted spoon and place in a colander. Add the green beans to the boiling water and cook for 5 minutes after the water has come back to the boil, then remove with a slotted spoon to the colander. Keep the water to one side as this is going to be part of the soup.

Cook the macaroni in a separate pan of boiling salted water for 3 minutes less than the packet suggests, then drain and keep to one side.

To make the pesto, crush the half garlic clove with a little salt to a fine paste in a pestle and mortar. Add the basil and crush until the leaves become a pulp, then add the pine nuts and crush to a paste. Stir in the parmesan, followed by the water. Mix until emulsified, then slowly add the olive oil. Keep to one side.

Add 1.5 litres (50fl oz) of the vegetable cooking water to the pan with the soup base. Bring to a simmer, then add the borlotti beans and cook for 10 minutes so the potatoes are cooked through, and the soup starts to increase in flavour. Add the courgettes and green beans and cook gently for 5 minutes.

Take out a large cup of the soup and blitz with a slick blender to a fine purée, then add this back to the soup. Add the cooked macaroni and check the seasoning. Serve in warm soup bowls with a generous spoonful of fresh pesto in each bowl.

Green beans with butter, garlic and parsley

Serves 4 as a side dish

500g (1lb 2oz) fine
   green beans
100g (3½oz) unsalted butter
1 garlic clove, crushed to
   a paste with a little salt
2 tbsp chopped flat-leaf
   parsley
sea salt and freshly ground
   black pepper

My mother-in-law, Josselyne, has been making these green beans for many years, and this is probably the simplest and nicest way to serve them, especially when they are in season. The garlic butter with the parsley and the sweet, tender green beans is a magical combination that could be eaten on its own or as a side dish.

Add the green beans to a large saucepan of boiling salted water and cook for 5 minutes after the water has come back to the boil. Drain into a colander. Wash the pan and place back on the stove over a medium heat.

Add the butter and, when it has melted, add the crushed garlic in salt and the parsley, then add the green beans and cook slowly for 5 minutes, turning occasionally so the ingredients are mixed well together.

Check the seasoning: you probably will not need any salt as the garlic is already salty. Finish off with some black pepper and serve in a warm bowl in the middle of the table.

Borlotti beans with radicchio, grilled polenta and burrata

Serves 4

3 tbsp extra-virgin olive oil
1 red chilli, deseeded and
  finely chopped
1 tbsp balsamic vinegar
1 garlic clove, crushed to
  a paste with a little sea salt
2 medium radicchio heads,
  each cut into 8 wedges
2 x 400g (14oz) cans of
  borlotti beans, drained
  and rinsed
1 tbsp chopped flat-leaf
  parsley
150g (5½oz) burrata,
  finely chopped
sea salt and freshly ground
  black pepper

For the polenta
400ml (14fl oz) water
100g (3½oz) Bramata polenta
  (coarse cornmeal)
50g (1¾oz) unsalted butter
100g (3½oz) parmesan, grated

I have used canned borlotti beans in this chapter because they are reliable and easy to use. If you get hold of some dried beans or, better still, fresh, then use them here, as when cooked carefully they taste even better than the canned variety – and they will really shine in this recipe. Roasted radicchio and borlotti beans is a Veneto classic combination. The radicchio loses its bitterness when cooked and, with the addition of balsamic vinegar, becomes almost sweet-like. Grilled polenta works nicely, and with the addition of chopped burrata makes a lovely dish.

To make the polenta, bring the water to a boil in a saucepan, add a pinch of salt and, when simmering, add the polenta gradually and use a balloon whisk to stir it in; it's important you add it gradually, so the polenta can be dispersed evenly and will therefore cook properly. Once you have added all the polenta, turn down the heat and cook gently for 30 minutes, until the polenta is starting to come away from the edges of the pan. Pour into a straight-sided ceramic dish so the polenta is 2cm (¾in) thick. Leave to cool and set firm.

Preheat the oven to 180°C/160°C fan/350°F/Gas 4.

Once set, cut the polenta into 8 strips. Heat a griddle pan until very hot, then add the polenta slices. Leave for 4 minutes, without touching them, so that the polenta forms a crust (this will make it easier to flip and will also add flavour). Carefully turn over each slice and cook for 4 minutes on the other side. Take off the heat and place on an oven tray. Rub the butter on one side of each piece of grilled polenta and sprinkle over the parmesan. Place in the oven to keep warm.

In a large bowl, mix 1 tablespoon of the olive oil, the chilli, vinegar and crushed garlic in salt. Add the radicchio wedges and toss well to coat, then place in a single layer on a roasting tray lined with baking paper. Cover with foil and cook in the oven for 20 minutes, then remove the foil and cook for a further 5 minutes. Keep to one side.

Add the remaining 2 tablespoons of oil to a hot, medium saucepan, then add the borlotti beans, parsley and some salt and pepper and cook gently for 5 minutes. Keep warm.

Add two slices of polenta to each plate, spoon over some beans, then top with the radicchio and a dollop of chopped burrata.

Risotto with borlotti beans, radicchio and rosemary

Serves 4

2 tbsp extra-virgin olive oil
1 small red onion, finely
  chopped
2 celery stalks, finely chopped
350g (12oz) Carnaroli
  risotto rice
100ml (3½fl oz) sweet red
  wine or 50ml (1¾fl oz) port
1.5 litres (34fl oz) hot
  vegetable stock (see
  page 19 for homemade)
1 small radicchio head,
  shredded
1 x 400g (14oz) can of borlotti
  beans, drained and rinsed
75g (2½oz) unsalted butter
100g (3½oz) parmesan, finely
  grated, plus extra to serve
1 tsp chopped rosemary
sea salt and freshly ground
  black pepper

This is a really good combination of flavours and textures, even though it may sound a bit odd. I love the flavour of cooked radicchio in a risotto, as it keeps its bitter characteristic, but with the addition of the sweet wine, rosemary, parmesan and borlotti beans, it all comes together beautifully. Even if you are not a fan of radicchio, you must try this.

Add the oil to a hot, large, straight-sided saucepan, then add the onion and celery and cook gently over a medium heat for 3 minutes. Add the rice and keep cooking for a further 3 minutes, stirring all the time. Add the wine or port and stir until the liquid has evaporated. Start adding the stock, a ladleful at a time, so the rice is always just covered; keep doing this for 10 minutes over a medium heat so the risotto is bubbling away.

Add the shredded radicchio, borlotti beans and another ladleful of stock and cook for a further 6 minutes. Add enough stock so the risotto seems very wet, then add the butter, parmesan and rosemary, stirring thoroughly for 2 minutes.

Check the seasoning, place a tight-fitting lid on the pan and turn off the heat. Leave on the stove for 2 minutes, then take off the lid, give it a good stir and serve on warm plates or bowls, with extra parmesan and black pepper on top. The risotto should be creamy with a nice bite to the rice; the radicchio will have lost most of its bitter flavour and the beans will add a sweetness.

Mezze maniche with green beans and tomatoes

Serves 4

300g (10½oz) fine green
  beans, topped and tailed,
  then halved lengthways
3 tbsp extra-virgin olive oil,
  plus extra to serve
2 spring onions (scallions)
  or 1 small white onion,
  finely chopped
10 taggiasche or niçoise
  olives, pitted and roughly
  chopped
250g (9oz) datterini or cherry
  tomatoes, quartered
6 basil leaves, torn
25g (1oz) miniature capers
  in vinegar, drained
400g (14oz) dried mezze
  maniche or rigatoni pasta
50g (1¾oz) ricotta salata,
  grated
sea salt and freshly ground
  black pepper

Green beans in a pasta dish may not be an obvious choice, but, believe me, it is one of the best ways to use fine green beans. This is a no-nonsense, quick pasta dish that is tasty and easy to make. Don't add too much salt to the tomato sauce, as the capers, olives and ricotta salata will give out plenty. Summer cooking at its best.

Add the green beans to a medium saucepan of boiling salted water and cook for 5 minutes after the water has come back to the boil. Drain into a colander.

Heat the olive oil in a hot, large, non-stick frying pan, add the spring onions and cook over a low heat for 10 minutes until soft. Add the green beans, olives and tomatoes, cook gently for 5 minutes, then add the basil and capers. Leave to one side.

Cook the pasta in a large pan of boiling salted water for 3 minutes less than the packet suggests. Using a slotted spoon, remove the pasta from the water and add it directly to the frying pan with the green beans and tomatoes. Add a couple of ladlefuls of pasta cooking water and put the pan back over a medium heat for 3 minutes, stirring with a wooden spoon so the tomatoes and green beans are well mixed with the pasta and the sauce starts to emulsify.

Check the seasoning and add some black pepper. Serve in warm pasta bowls with some grated ricotta salata on top, and a little extra olive oil.

SQUASH

Onion squash with radicchio, lentils and rainbow chard

Serves 4 as a starter or side

1 medium onion squash,
 peeled, halved and deseeded
4 tbsp extra-virgin olive oil
1 garlic clove, finely chopped
1 tsp thyme leaves
2 radicchio heads, leaves
 separated
500g (1lb 2oz) rainbow chard,
 stems cut into 2cm (¾in)
 slices and leaves into 4cm
 (1½in) slices
juice of ½ lemon
100g (3½oz) dried Umbrian
 or Puy (French) lentils
sea salt and freshly ground
 black pepper

For the dressing
2 red chillies, deseeded and
 finely chopped
1 tsp chopped flat-leaf parsley
1 tbsp best-quality (thick
 density) aged balsamic
 vinegar
3 tbsp extra-virgin olive oil

Roasted onion squash with rainbow chard and blanched radicchio is a lovely combination of colours and flavours, making for a perfect warm autumn salad. The balsamic vinegar dressing brings the combination of vegetables to life, and the lentils make it much more of a complete meal.

Preheat the oven to 180°C/160°C fan/350°F/Gas 4.

Cut the onion squash into 2cm (¾in) half-moon wedges and place in a large bowl with 2 tablespoons of the olive oil, the garlic, thyme and some salt and black pepper. Mix well and lay the squash flat in a roasting tin lined with baking paper. Cover with foil so there are no gaps and cook in the oven for 35 minutes. Remove the foil, turn the squash over and cook for a further 10 minutes so the squash gets a nice golden colour and goes slightly crispy. Remove from the oven and leave to cool slightly.

Add the radicchio leaves to a pan of boiling salted water and cook for 3 minutes after the water has come back to the boil. Drain into a colander and leave to cool. Take a large, clean tea (dish) towel and place the radicchio leaves on it, roll into a sausage shape and squeeze gently to fully dry the radicchio.

Add the chard stems to a pan of boiling salted water and cook for 2 minutes, then add the chard leaves and cook for a further 3 minutes. Drain into a colander and leave to cool. When cool, take a few sheets of kitchen paper and push down on the rainbow chard and stalks, to remove excess water.

In a large bowl, mix the radicchio and rainbow chard together with salt, black pepper, the remaining 2 tablespoons of olive oil and the lemon juice. The radicchio will change colour to a bright crimson when the lemon juice touches it.

Add the lentils to a small saucepan, add water to come 5cm (2in) above the level of the lentils, and cook for 20 minutes or until the lentils are tender and have a little bite. Drain and season with salt and black pepper.

Place the warm squash on a platter, then scatter over the chard and radicchio, and then the warm lentils. Stir together the dressing ingredients, then drizzle this over the salad. Serve in the middle of the table to share.

Squash, onion and rocket frittata with ricotta and parmesan

Serves 4

2 tbsp extra-virgin olive oil
1 medium red onion,
  finely sliced
1 tsp thyme leaves
600g (1lb 5oz) butternut
  squash, peeled and cut into
  roughly 2cm (¾in) pieces
6 eggs
150g (5½oz) ricotta
100g (3½oz) parmesan, grated
100g (3½oz) wild rocket
  (arugula), roughly chopped
1 tsp marjoram leaves,
  chopped
25g (1oz) butter
sea salt and freshly ground
  black pepper

Frittatas are always simple crowd pleasers – and the bright orange colour of squash makes this frittata look lovely and golden. You could use other squash here, like onion squash, but butternut is easy to find and is usually consistent in colour and flavour. Make sure the squash is cooked through and really soft before constructing the frittata.

Preheat the oven to 180°C/160°C fan/350°F/Gas 4.

Add the olive oil to a hot, large non-stick, ovenproof frying pan, and add the onion, thyme and a good pinch of salt. Cook over a medium heat for 5 minutes, stirring occasionally. Add the squash, turn down the heat and place a tight-fitting lid on the pan. Cook for 15 minutes, stirring from time to time. When the squash and onions are soft and have become a little mashed, remove them from the pan and place on a plate to cool down.

Break the eggs into a large bowl and whisk thoroughly so they become one colour. Add the ricotta, parmesan, rocket, marjoram, and some salt and black pepper. Whisk all the ingredients together so they are emulsified, then stir in the cooled squash and onion mixture.

Wash the frying pan you used to cook the squash and place over a medium heat. Add the butter and wait for it to melt then foam, then add the egg mixture, confidently in one go. Don't touch the pan for 2 minutes, so the mixture starts to set on the outside. Give it a little shake, then place in the oven for 10 minutes. The frittata should be set firm, so give it a wiggle to check there is no wetness in the middle.

Remove from the oven and place the pan on a wire rack to cool for 10 minutes. When you are ready to turn the frittata out of the pan, warm the pan over a medium heat for 1 minute and place a large plate on top of the pan. Using a tea (dish) towel or oven gloves, carefully and swiftly invert the frittata onto the plate.

Serve with bitter leaves with a mustard and honey dressing.

Fritto of squash, Jerusalem artichoke and cauliflower

Serves 4 as a starter

2 medium cauliflowers, florets
  cut from the stem
1 medium butternut squash,
  peeled
8 large Jerusalem artichokes
juice of ½ lemon
750ml (25fl oz) sunflower oil
150g (5½oz) tipo 00 flour
sea salt

For the sauce
2 large medium-hot red
  chillies, deseeded and
  finely chopped
20 mint leaves, finely chopped
1 tbsp honey
2 tbsp red wine vinegar
1 garlic clove, crushed to
  a paste with a little sea salt

For the batter
200g (7oz) tipo 00 flour
50ml (1¾fl oz) extra-virgin
  olive oil
1 egg white, beaten

I love making these fried vegetables at home; they all have a sweet taste and go nicely with the chilli, mint and vinegar. The different textures of the vegetables make for a very interesting fritto misto – perfect for a party snack.

Whisk all the sauce ingredients in a bowl. Keep to one side.

To make the batter, add the flour to a large bowl with the olive oil and egg white, and whisk in enough warm water to achieve a batter the same consistency as runny honey. If you add too much water and the batter seems too thin, add another tablespoon of flour. Cover and place in the fridge for 15 minutes.

Add the cauliflower florets to a pan of boiling salted water and cook for 5 minutes after the water has come back to the boil. Drain into a colander and keep to one side.

Halve the peeled butternut squash and scoop out the seeds and any stringy bits. Place the halves flat-side down on a chopping board and cut into roughly 1cm (½in) slices. Keep to one side.

Peel the Jerusalem artichokes and place straight in a bowl of cold water with the lemon juice. Leave for 10 minutes, then cut each in half lengthways. Place flat-side down on a chopping board and cut into roughly 1cm (½in) slices.

Add the sunflower oil to a large non-stick frying pan and place over a medium heat. Preheat the oven to 150°C/130°C fan/ 300°F/Gas 2.

Add the flour to a large bowl, then add the sliced squash and artichokes, and the cooked cauliflower. With your hands, toss the vegetables in the flour so they are lightly coated, then place them on a tray, ready to dip into the batter.

Turn the heat up on the oil, then dip a cauliflower floret into the batter and place it in the hot oil to test the heat – it should start to bubble within a few seconds. When the oil is hot enough, in batches, start dipping the vegetables into the batter and placing them in the hot oil, making sure you don't overcrowd the pan. Cook until lightly golden, then remove them with a slotted spoon and place on some kitchen paper to absorb any excess oil. Repeat until you have fried all the vegetables, then transfer them to an oven tray and place into the oven for a few minutes.

Arrange the hot, fried vegetables on a large platter, drizzle over the chilli mint sauce, sprinkle over some salt and serve.

Crown Prince squash soup with smoked scamorza crostini

Serves 8

4 tbsp extra-virgin olive oil
1kg (2lb 3oz) Crown Prince
   squash, peeled, deseeded
   and cut into 2cm (¾in)
   pieces
1 garlic clove, finely chopped
1 tsp thyme leaves
100g (3½oz) dried Umbrian
   or Puy (French) lentils
2 medium leeks, sliced into
   1cm (½in) rounds
2 medium carrots, peeled and
   finely chopped
4 celery stalks, finely chopped
1 tsp chopped rosemary
180g (6¼oz) vacuum-packed
   chestnuts, finely chopped
2 litres (68fl oz) boiling water
100ml (3½fl oz) crème fraîche,
   plus extra to serve
1 tbsp chopped flat-leaf
   parsley
sea salt and freshly ground
   black pepper

For the crostini
8 slices of dry baguette,
   2cm (½in) thick
extra-virgin olive oil,
   for drizzling
1 garlic clove, peeled
8 slices of smoked scamorza

Crown Prince squash has a matt grey-green skin and a bright orange, dry flesh that is excellent in soups and pasta fillings. Seeing this squash and chestnuts in shops is the first sign of winter – and this soup is a perfect comforting bowl of goodness for this cold season. The smoked scamorza crostini make the soup even better, adding a smoky, creamy bite.

Preheat the oven to 180°C/160°C fan/350°F/Gas 4.

Add 2 tablespoons of the olive oil to a large bowl and add the squash, garlic and thyme, stirring to coat the squash. Line a roasting tray with baking paper and spread the squash out in an even layer. Cover tightly with foil and cook for 35 minutes. Remove the foil and cook for a further 5 minutes, so the squash dries out a bit and gets a little colour. Leave to one side.

Add the lentils to a small saucepan and add water to come 5cm (2in) above the level of the lentils. Cook for 20 minutes or until tender and the lentils have a little bite. Drain and put to one side.

Add the remaining 2 tablespoons of olive oil to a hot, large saucepan, add the leeks, carrots, celery, rosemary and a good pinch of salt. Cook for 15 minutes so all the vegetables are soft. Add the chestnuts and roasted squash and cook for 5 minutes so the squash becomes very soft. Add the boiling water and lentils and cook over a low heat for 20 minutes. Add salt and black pepper to taste, then stir through the crème fraîche and parsley. Take out a cupful of the soup and blitz with a stick blender, then pour this back in the saucepan with the rest of the soup; this will make the soup really creamy. Keep warm to one side.

Place the baguette slices on a roasting tray, drizzle a little olive oil onto each slice and place in the oven for 5 minutes. Flip the slices, rub each with the garlic clove, then top with a slice of smoked scamorza. Return to the oven until the cheese has melted.

Serve the soup in warm bowls with a dollop of crème fraîche in each and the melted smoked scamorza crostini on the side.

Squash and potato gnocchi with sage butter and truffle cream

Serves 6

1 tbsp extra-virgin olive oil
300g (10½oz) peeled and
  cubed butternut squash
1kg (2lb 3oz) red potatoes,
  peeled
350g (12oz) tipo 00 flour,
  plus extra for dusting
2 eggs, beaten
sea salt and freshly ground
  black pepper
parmesan, grated, to serve

For the black truffle cream
250ml (9fl oz) single
  (light) cream
1 garlic clove, crushed to
  a paste with a little sea salt
75g (2½oz) parmesan, grated
50g (1¾oz) black truffle, finely
  grated (see intro), or use
  minced from a jar

For the brown butter
75g (2½oz) unsalted butter
10 sage leaves

Potato gnocchi is always good, but this combination of flavours takes the humble potato and butternut squash to new heights. The truffle cream is something special – a combination of cooked cream, parmesan and black truffle. Finding black truffle is challenging, but if you get one then you must try this recipe. I find grating it on a Microplane is the best way to get maximum flavour from the truffle. The brown butter and crispy sage are the finishing touches that will make you want to lick the bowl clean.

Preheat the oven to 180°C/160°C fan/350°F/Gas 4.

Add the olive oil to a baking dish, then add the cubed squash with some salt and black pepper. Cover tightly with foil and cook in the oven for 25 minutes, then remove the foil and cook for a further 5 minutes, so the squash dries out a little. Take out of the oven and leave to one side.

Place the potatoes in a large pot of water and add 1 teaspoon of salt. Bring to the boil and cook for 30–40 minutes, depending on the size of the potatoes. When you can push a knife through a potato, remove them with a slotted spoon and pass through a mouli or potato ricer (it's best to crush them when hot to allow as much steam as possible to escape), along with the squash.

Place the potato and roasted squash mash on a large board or tray with the flour. When the mash has cooled a little, use your hands to combine it with the flour and beaten eggs, so you have a smooth orange ball. If the mixture feels too wet, add a little extra flour.

Divide into quarters and, using the palms of your hands and fingers, roll each into a long sausage about 3cm (1¼in) thick. Cut each sausage into 3cm (1¼in) pieces using a blunt knife, then push each piece down onto the back of a dinner fork, rolling the gnocchi so they have deep ridges on them (the ridges help the sauce cling to the gnocchi).

Place the gnocchi in a single layer on a tray, cover with baking paper (not cling film/plastic wrap, as this makes them wet and sticky) and place in the fridge for 1 hour.

Continued overleaf

Squash and potato gnocchi with sage butter and truffle cream
continued

Next, make the truffle cream. Add the cream to a hot, large non-stick frying pan, bring to a simmer, then add the crushed garlic in salt and the parmesan. Shake the pan or stir with a wooden spoon so all the ingredients emulsify, then take off the heat and stir in the finely grated or minced black truffle. Leave to one side.

To make the brown butter, place the butter and sage in a small saucepan over a low heat until the butter goes a light golden brown and the sage starts to go crispy. Strain through a fine sieve with a small bowl underneath to collect the brown butter. Place the sage leaves on some kitchen paper. Keep to one side.

Add the gnocchi to a large pan of boiling salted water. When they rise to the top, remove them with a slotted spoon and add them to the truffle cream in the frying pan. Place the pan over a medium heat and add a couple of ladlefuls of the gnocchi cooking water. Shake the pan so the sauce starts to emulsify with the gnocchi; this will take about 3 minutes.

When you are happy that the sauce is coating the gnocchi, serve in warm pasta bowls. Spoon over a drizzle of brown butter, top with a few leaves of crispy sage, then finish with some black pepper and grated parmesan.

Squash and ricotta tortellini with porcini and thyme sauce

Serves 8 as a starter

For the pasta dough
350g (12oz) tipo 00 flour
25g (1oz) fine semolina flour,
  plus 50g (1³⁄₄oz) for dusting
2 whole eggs plus 4 egg
  yolks, beaten together
2 tbsp water

For the filling
800g (1lb 12oz) butternut
  squash, peeled and cut
  roughly into 2cm (³⁄₄in)
  pieces
2 tbsp extra-virgin olive oil
1 garlic clove, finely chopped
1 tsp chopped marjoram
  leaves
250g (9oz) ricotta, drained
  and squeezed in a cloth
  to remove excess water
100g (3¹⁄₂oz) parmesan, finely
  grated, plus extra to serve
sea salt and freshly ground
  black pepper

For the porcini and thyme sauce
20g (³⁄₄oz) dried porcini
  mushrooms, soaked in
  250ml (9fl oz) hot water
  for 15 minutes
75g (2¹⁄₂oz) butter
1 garlic clove, finely chopped
1 tsp thyme leaves

Stuffed fresh pasta is always a treat, especially with a squash filling. The porcini mushroom and thyme sauce complements the tortellini, giving a rich mushroom flavour to the dish. Make sure the squash is dry when you mix it with the ricotta and, more importantly, squeeze out any excess water from the ricotta, as it tends to be very wet – even if it doesn't look wet you will be surprised how much water comes out when you squeeze it through a cloth.

Make the pasta dough. Combine both flours in a large bowl and add the beaten eggs and water. Mix with a fork to combine, then use your hands to form a dough. Once the dough is smooth, divide into quarters, wrap in cling film (plastic wrap) and rest in the fridge for 20 minutes.

Preheat the oven to 180°C/160°C fan/350°F/Gas 4.

Add the squash to a large bowl with the olive oil, garlic, marjoram and some salt and black pepper. Mix well so the squash is well coated. Line a roasting tin with baking paper and spread the squash out evenly. Cover tightly with foil and cook in the oven for 30 minutes. Remove the foil, then cook for a further 5 minutes so the butternut squash is dry. Leave to cool.

When the roasted squash has cooled down, mix it in a large bowl with the ricotta and parmesan, using a wooden spoon to beat the mixture until there are no large pieces of squash. Add salt and black pepper to taste and leave to one side.

Take one of the pieces of pasta and, using a rolling pin, roll until the pasta dough is thin enough to go through the rollers on your pasta machine. Place one end in the machine on the widest setting and roll it through the machine. Fold the pasta in half and roll again. Repeat 4 times for each quarter of pasta. This process makes the pasta more elastic and durable.

Now roll each quarter of pasta through the machine into long sheets – when you can see the silhouette of your hand behind the pasta, it is thin enough.

When you have rolled all the pasta, you can start making the tortellini. Have the filling mixture ready in a bowl, with a teaspoon.

Continued overleaf

Place a pasta sheet on the work surface with some extra flour to stop it sticking. Using an 8–10cm (3¼–4in) round cutter, cut rounds of the pasta. Place a teaspoon of filling mixture in the middle of each round and, using a spray bottle or your finger, wet the pasta. Fold over the pasta and seal the edges so you now have a half-moon shape that is sealed with no gaps. Gently roll over the filled part of the pasta then bring the two sides together and pinch tightly so the pasta edges stay together. Repeat this process until you have used all the pasta and filling.

Place the tortellini on a tray dusted with semolina and leave to dry out for 1 hour before cooking; this will give the pasta a better bite. Kept in the fridge, they can last for up to 3 days, but do not cover them with cling film (plastic wrap) as this will make the pasta go soggy – cover with baking paper with a large elastic band on each end of the tray to hold it in place. This pasta also freezes well.

To make the sauce, drain the porcini mushrooms, reserving the soaking liquid. Finely chop the porcini and strain the soaking liquid through a fine sieve or a paper coffee filter to remove any grit. Set the chopped porcini and strained liquid to one side.

Add half the butter to a small saucepan over a medium heat, then add the garlic, thyme, chopped porcini and the soaking liquid. Cook until the liquid has evaporated by half, then stir in the remaining butter and some salt and black pepper and leave to one side.

Add the tortellini one at a time to a large pan of boiling salted water and cook for 4 minutes. Remove with a slotted spoon and place in a large non-stick frying pan with the porcini mushroom sauce. Add a ladleful of the pasta cooking water and check the seasoning. Give the pan a shake, so the starch from the pasta thickens up the sauce and they become emulsified; this will take a couple of minutes.

Serve in warm bowls, with a little extra grated parmesan on the side.

Roasted onion squash, fennel, leeks, carrot and turnips

Serves 4 as a starter or side

1 medium onion squash
or butternut squash

5 tbsp extra-virgin olive oil

2 tsp thyme leaves

1 garlic bulb, cloves separated

2 fennel bulbs, quartered

2 medium leeks, sliced into
3cm (1¼in) rounds

6 carrots, peeled and halved
lengthways

2 medium Cyprus potatoes,
peeled and cut into 2cm
(¾in) wedges

4 turnips, the size of a golf
ball, halved

sea salt and freshly ground
black pepper

Onion squash has its name because it looks like an onion. The skin is bright orange, as is the flesh. It's one of the first squashes available in early September and has many culinary uses: it's great in soups, pasta fillings, and simply roasted like in this recipe. The texture of onion squash when cooked is very nice as it remains firm but is not dry like many other squashes. I would eat this with a green salad with a shallot and red wine vinegar dressing.

Preheat the oven to 180°C/160°C fan/350°F/Gas 4.

Peel the squash, cut in half and scoop out the seeds and any stringy bits. Cut the squash into to 2cm (¾in) wedges.

Add the olive oil, thyme, garlic cloves, fennel, leeks, carrots, potatoes, turnips and squash to a large bowl. Add some salt and black pepper and mix well so all the vegetables are coated in olive oil.

Place the prepared vegetables in a roasting tin lined with baking paper. Make sure all the vegetables are evenly spread out and not too much on top of each other. Cover with foil and bake in the oven for 40 minutes. Check the vegetables are cooked by putting a sharp knife through a potato; there should be no resistance. Remove the foil and cook for a further 10 minutes in the oven to allow the vegetables to get a little colour.

Allow the vegetables to rest for 5 minutes, then tip them into a warm serving dish. Serve as a side dish or as part of a spread.

Butternut squash and celeriac al forno

Serves 8

2 medium butternut squash
2 medium celeriac
   (celery root)
2 tbsp extra-virgin olive oil
2 tsp thyme leaves
250ml (9fl oz) whole milk
500ml (17fl oz) single
   (light) cream
50g (1³⁄₄oz) soft butter
1 garlic clove, crushed to
   a paste with a little sea salt
100g (3¹⁄₂oz) breadcrumbs
75g (2¹⁄₂oz) parmesan, grated
sea salt and freshly ground
   black pepper

A hearty and warming dish, this recipe is really simple to make but feels wonderfully indulgent, with the sweetness from the squash and celeriac cutting through the richness of the cream. Serve with some garlicky green beans for dinner, or as a side dish.

Preheat the oven to 180°C/160°C fan/350°F/Gas 4.

Peel the butternut squash, then cut each in half lengthways and scoop out the seeds and any stringy bits. Place the 4 halves flat-side down on a chopping board and, with a very sharp knife, cut into 1cm (½in) slices (don't worry if they are not perfect). Keep to one side.

Peel the celeriac and cut each in half. Place flat-side down on the chopping board and again, cut into 1cm (½in) slices; again, they don't have to be the perfect thickness. Mix the slices of squash and celeriac in a large bowl with the olive oil, half the thyme and some salt and black pepper. Toss well so the thyme sticks to the squash and celeriac. Keep to one side.

Mix the milk and cream together in a jug (pitcher).

In a small bowl, mix together the butter and crushed garlic in salt and spread this over the insides of a large baking dish. Add a layer of celeriac and squash slices, then pour over some of the cream and milk mixture. Add another layer of celeriac and squash, then another of milk and cream, repeating until you have used all the celeriac and squash, and milk and cream mixture. Cover tightly with baking paper and a layer of foil, making sure there are no gaps. Place in the oven and cook for 1 hour.

Meanwhile, mix the breadcrumbs, parmesan and remaining thyme together in a bowl and keep to one side.

Check the celeriac and squash are cooked by pushing a sharp knife through the foil; if there is no resistance then they are cooked. Remove the foil and evenly scatter over the breadcrumb mixture. Place back in the oven for a further 15 minutes so the breadcrumbs turn a light golden brown. Remove from the oven and leave to stand for 20 minutes before serving.

Squash, leek, mascarpone and porcini sauce with pappardelle

Serves 4 as a starter

3 tbsp extra-virgin olive oil
400g (14oz) butternut squash,
 peeled and cut into roughly
 2cm (¾in) pieces
2 medium leeks, sliced into
 1cm (½in) rounds
1 tsp thyme leaves
20g (¾oz) dried porcini
 mushrooms, soaked in
 hot water for 15 minutes
100g (3½oz) mascarpone
250g (9oz) dried pappardelle
sea salt and freshly ground
 black pepper
parmesan, grated, to serve

Pappardelle is the perfect pasta for this sauce as the wide ribbons hold it perfectly. Good-quality porcini mushrooms tend to not have much grit, but make sure you check them after being soaked. I love the taste of slow-cooked leeks, butternut squash and thyme – adding mascarpone only makes this combination even better.

Add the olive oil to a large non-stick frying pan over a medium heat, then add the squash, leeks, thyme and a good pinch of salt. Place a tight-fitting lid on the frying pan and cook slowly for 20 minutes, stirring occasionally. The squash and leeks will soften and reduce substantially.

Chop the soaked porcini to a fine pulp and strain the soaking liquid through a piece of kitchen paper or a paper coffee filter. Add the porcini and strained liquid to the squash and leeks and cook for a further 5 minutes over a low heat. Add the mascarpone and check the seasoning, giving the sauce a stir so the mascarpone melts and the sauce is creamy.

Cook the pappardelle in a pan of boiling salted water for 1 minute less than the packet suggests, then remove with a pair of tongs and add to the frying pan with the sauce. Add 2 ladlefuls of pasta cooking water and cook for a further 2 minutes so the sauce coats the pasta.

Check the seasoning and serve in warm pasta bowls with parmesan and black pepper.

Butternut squash and whisky ice cream

Serves 8

600g (1lb 5oz) peeled, cubed
  butternut squash
750ml (25fl oz) whole milk
1 vanilla pod (bean), halved
  lengthways and seeds
  scraped out
zest of 1 orange
2 tbsp honey, plus extra
  to serve
2 x 400ml (14fl oz) cans of
  coconut cream
75ml (2¼fl oz) whisky, plus
  extra to serve

This may sound a bit odd, but believe me it really does taste good. I first tasted something like this in a restaurant in Bangkok – it didn't have whisky in it but I think the whisky notes make the combination of flavours come together. This is a very rich ice cream so don't serve too much – it's perfect as a sweet mouthful at the end of a meal.

Add the squash, milk and vanilla seeds to a saucepan and cook, covered, over a low heat for 25 minutes or until you can easily put a sharp knife through the squash. Take off the heat and tip into a bowl. Using a stick blender, blend to a purée.

Add the orange zest, honey, coconut cream and whisky to the purée and mix well so all the ingredients are combined. Leave to cool in the fridge for 1 hour, then take out of the fridge and, using the stick blender, whisk the mixture so it becomes more aerated. Place in a suitable shallow freezer container that has a lid and pop in the freezer overnight.

Serve in small, cold glasses from the freezer with a drizzle of honey and a shot of whisky on top for a real treat.

POTATOES

Celeriac, potato and turnip rosti

Serves 4

1 small celeriac (celery root), peeled
3 golf-ball-sized turnips, tops removed
4 medium Désirée or Cyprus potatoes, peeled
1 garlic clove, crushed to a paste with a little sea salt
1 tsp thyme leaves
4 tbsp sunflower oil
4 fried eggs, to serve

I have been making rosti potatoes since my first job at Chez Max many moons ago. I remember when Max first taught me how to make them, I was so worried I would muck them up. Well, I was right – the first couple I made were not worthy of his dining room, to put it mildly. I got better with practice and, as with most things, 'practice makes perfect'.

My children love a potato rosti and will always ask for one if there is a chance of a late breakfast on offer. This recipe uses other vegetables as well as potatoes, making it a very tasty combination. The trick is to cook it over a low heat, otherwise the turnips will brown before the other ingredients are cooked through. Take your time and cook it slowly.

Preheat the oven to 180°C/160°C fan/350°F/Gas 4.

Using the largest holes on a box grater, grate the celeriac and place in a large bowl. Do the same with the turnips and finally the potatoes. Mix all the ingredients together, then add the crushed garlic in salt and the thyme. Mix thoroughly.

Add the sunflower oil to a hot, large non-stick, ovenproof frying pan, then add the grated vegetable mixture in one go. Leave for a couple of minutes, then push them down with a wooden spoon in the middle and to the sides so the vegetables start taking the shape of the frying pan. Turn the heat to low and cook for 5 minutes, then push down on the edges and the middle again so the vegetables are covering the whole base of the pan. Turn the heat up for a few seconds and shake the pan to ensure it is not sticking. With one confident but careful motion, turn over the rosti, then turn down the heat to low.

Cook for 5 minutes, then transfer to the oven and cook for a further 10 minutes. Take the pan out and place a chopping board on top, then, using a tea (dish) towel or oven gloves, invert the rosti onto the chopping board. Leave for 5 minutes before serving in quarters for breakfast with a fried egg on top, or by itself as a side.

Vegetable salad with salsa verde

Serves 4 as a starter

1kg (2lb 3oz) Ratte or
  Charlotte potatoes
12 baby carrots, scrubbed
8 thick asparagus spears,
  tough ends removed
2 heads of spring (collard)
  greens, washed and
  quartered lengthways
8 baby leeks, ends removed
  (ensure there is no grit)
sea salt and freshly ground
  black pepper

For the salsa verde
100g (3½oz) flat-leaf parsley
100g (3½oz) wild rocket
  (arugula)
50g (1¾oz) basil leaves
25g (1oz) mint leaves
1 tbsp miniature capers
  in vinegar, drained
1 tsp Dijon mustard
4 tbsp extra-virgin olive oil

This is a salad I have been making at home for years, especially when the new season's asparagus comes in. Ratte potatoes are long, root-looking potatoes that are incredibly waxy so are perfect for this recipe. The salsa verde seasons the vegetables and brings all the flavours together. Make sure all the vegetables are dry before you add the salsa verde, so the end result doesn't become watery.

Place all the salsa verde ingredients except the mustard and oil on a chopping board. Using a big knife, finely chop all the herbs, and then the capers, together on the board. Combine in a bowl with the mustard and olive oil. Check the seasoning and set aside.

Wash the potatoes in cold water and rub the skins with a clean scourer, to remove the outer skin. Rinse again, then place in a saucepan of water with a teaspoon of salt. Cook over a medium heat for 25 minutes. Check they are cooked by pushing a sharp knife through one; if there is no resistance they are ready. Drain in a colander and leave to cool.

Add the carrots to a large pan of boiling salted water and cook for 4 minutes after the water has come back to the boil. Remove with a slotted spoon and place in a colander to cool. Add the asparagus to the boiling water and cook for 4 minutes after the water has come back to the boil. Remove with a slotted spoon and place in the colander with the carrots. Add the spring green quarters to the boiling water and cook for 4 minutes after the water has come back to the boil – remove to the colander. Now add the leeks and cook for 4 minutes after the water has come back to the boil, then remove to the colander to cool.

When all the vegetables have cooled to room temperature, place them on a few sheets of kitchen paper, and then cover with more sheets of kitchen paper, to absorb any excess water. This is important; if the vegetables are not dried, the end result will not be as delicious.

Cut the cooked potatoes in half and keep them to one side. Cut the asparagus spears in half lengthways, and do the same with the leeks.

Add half the salsa verde to a large bowl, then add all the vegetables. With your hands, toss gently so all the vegetables are covered in some salsa verde, adding salt if needed, and a little black pepper. Serve on a large plate in the middle of the table with the remaining salsa verde drizzled over the top.

Grated potato and onion fritters with salsa verde

Makes 12

600g (1lb 5oz) Désirée
  or Cyprus potatoes, grated
1 egg, beaten
2 red onions, finely sliced
75g (2½oz) cornflour
  (cornstarch)
150ml (5fl oz) sunflower oil
sea salt and freshly ground
  black pepper
lemon wedges, to serve

For the salsa verde
100g (3½oz) flat-leaf parsley
100g (3½oz) wild rocket
  (arugula)
50g (1¾oz) basil leaves
25g (1oz) mint leaves
1 tbsp miniature capers
  in vinegar, drained
1 tsp Dijon mustard
4 tbsp extra-virgin olive oil

This recipe is a variation on one of my mother-in-law Josselyne's classic dishes. She calls them potato latkes, and from the first time I ate one I wanted another. I have used salsa verde to drizzle on top of each fritter, making them fresh and tangy.

To make the salsa verde, place all the ingredients except the mustard and oil on a chopping board. Using a large knife, finely chop all the herbs, and then the capers, together on the board. Place in a bowl and mix together with the mustard and olive oil. Check the seasoning and keep to one side.

Preheat the oven to 150°C/130°C fan/300°F/Gas 2.

Place the grated potatoes in a tea (dish) towel and squeeze, so all the water is removed.

Add the beaten egg to a large bowl with the red onions, grated potatoes and cornflour, mix well and season with salt and black pepper.

Heat the sunflower oil in a large frying pan until it reads 160°C/320°F on a cooking thermometer, or a small piece of bread dropped in the oil sizzles immediately.

Using a slotted spoon, and in batches so you don't overcrowd the pan, place spoonfuls of the potato and egg mixture into the hot oil. Leave to set and cook for 3 minutes, then gently turn and cook for a further 2 minutes, until all sides are golden brown. Remove each fritter with a slotted spoon and place on a wire rack. Keep the fritters warm in the oven.

Place the hot fritters on a serving plate lined with baking paper, with lemon wedges to squeeze over and the salsa verde on the side to dip and drizzle.

Roasted sweet potato and zucchini risotto

Serves 4

500g (1lb 2oz) sweet potatoes,
 peeled and cut into roughly
 2cm (¾in) cubes
6 tbsp extra-virgin olive oil
1 tsp thyme leaves
1 garlic clove, sliced
4 basil leaves
3 medium courgettes
 (zucchini), sliced into
 5mm (¼in) rounds
100g (3½oz) unsalted butter
8 sage leaves
2 celery stalks, finely chopped
1 red onion, finely chopped
350g (12oz) Carnaroli
 risotto rice
100ml (3½fl oz) dry white wine
1.5 litres (50fl oz) hot
 vegetable stock (see
 page 19 for homemade)
75g (2½oz) parmesan, grated
100g (3½oz) smoked
 scamorza, grated
sea salt and freshly ground
 black pepper

Sweet potatoes are very much like a squash in flavour but are a bit drier in texture. This risotto is creamy and sweet, with the added flavour of smoked scamorza, which makes the whole bowlful utterly delicious. It is finished off with some brown butter and sage, which always goes so nicely with squash or sweet potatoes.

Preheat the oven to 180°C/160°C fan/350°F/Gas 4.

Toss the sweet potatoes in a bowl with 2 tablespoons of the olive oil, the thyme, and some salt and pepper. Tip out onto a roasting tray lined with baking paper, then cover tightly with foil and roast for 25 minutes. Remove the foil and check the sweet potatoes are cooked with a sharp knife; if there is no resistance, they are cooked. Return to the oven for 5 minutes, then set aside.

Add 2 tablespoons of the olive oil to a hot, medium saucepan, with the garlic, basil, courgettes and a good pinch of salt. Cover with a lid and cook over a medium heat for 10 minutes. Remove the lid and cook for a further 5 minutes so the courgettes become soft and a little caramelized. Take off the heat.

To make the brown butter, add 75g (2½oz) of the butter to a hot, small saucepan, add the sage and cook over a very low heat for 10 minutes, until the sage turns crispy and the butter is a nutty brown colour. Remove the crispy sage and place on some kitchen paper. Take the brown butter off the heat and keep to one side.

Add the remaining 2 tablespoons of olive oil to a hot, large, straight-sided saucepan and add the celery and red onion. Cook for 3 minutes, then add the rice and cook for a further 3 minutes so the rice absorbs the olive oil and goes translucent. Add the wine and cook until it is absorbed, then start adding the vegetable stock, a ladleful at a time, so the rice is always just covered. Continue for 10 minutes over a medium heat so the rice is bubbling away.

Add the cooked courgettes and enough stock so the risotto seems very wet, and cook for another 4 minutes. Add the roasted sweet potatoes and cook for another 2 minutes, then add the parmesan and smoked scamorza and the remaining butter. Stir vigorously for 2 minutes so the cheeses melt and the risotto becomes really emulsified. Check the seasoning, place a lid on the pan, take off the heat and leave for 2 minutes.

Take off the lid, give the risotto a good stir and serve in warm bowls, with a drizzle of the brown butter and some crispy sage leaves on top. Finish off with black pepper.

Ciambotta

Serves 6

6 tbsp extra-virgin olive oil,
  plus extra to serve
2 red onions, finely sliced
1 garlic clove, finely sliced
4 celery stalks, finely sliced
2 red (bell) peppers,
  deseeded and cut into
  2cm (¾in) pieces
3 medium courgettes, halved
  lengthways and cut into
  2cm (¾in) half-moon slices
600ml (20fl oz) tomato passata
  (strained tomatoes)
4 medium Désirée, Cyprus
  or any red potato, peeled
  and cut into roughly 2cm
  (¾in) pieces
250g (9oz) fine green beans,
  topped and tailed, then
  halved
4 medium aubergines
  (eggplants), cut into
  roughly 2cm (¾in) pieces
8 basil leaves, torn, plus extra
  to serve
1 red chilli, finely chopped
sea salt and freshly ground
  black pepper

Ciambotta is a southern Italian vegetable stew, halfway between Sicilian caponata and Provençal ratatouille. The difference is it includes potatoes and green beans, which makes it much more vegetable-stew-like. I first cooked this when I was doing research for our regional menu of Campania – I had cooked a few vegetable stews like it before but this is the real deal. It's important to use Désirée potatoes, or any potato that doesn't break up during the cooking.

Preheat the oven to 180°C/160°C fan/350°F/Gas 4.

Add 3 tablespoons of the olive oil to a hot, large saucepan, then add the red onions, garlic, celery, red pepper and a good pinch of salt. Cook over a medium heat for 15 minutes with a lid on so everything steams slightly and becomes soft. Add the courgettes and cook for a further 5 minutes, then add the passata and cook over a low heat for 20 minutes.

While the tomato is reducing, cook the potatoes in a pan of salted water until a sharp knife goes through them easily. Drain in a colander and keep to one side.

Add the green beans to a saucepan of boiling salted water and cook for 4 minutes after the water has come back to the boil. Drain in a colander and keep to one side.

Add the remaining 3 tablespoons of olive oil to a large bowl then add the aubergines and a good pinch of salt. Toss together so the aubergines absorb the oil. Place on a roasting tray lined with baking paper and cook in the oven for 15 minutes. Check that the aubergines are cooked: if a sharp knife goes through with no resistance, they are ready.

Add the cooked potatoes, green beans and aubergines to the pan of peppers and courgettes, and stir together gently so the vegetables don't break up too much. Add the basil and red chilli, stir again and check the seasoning.

Place the ciambotta on a large serving plate or dish, with extra basil, black pepper and a generous drizzle of olive oil on top.

Potato cjarson with peas, asparagus and butter

Serves 4 a starter

100g (3½oz) podded fresh
  peas or frozen petits pois
250g (9oz) asparagus spears,
  tough ends removed, sliced
  at an angle
50g (1¾oz) unsalted butter
sea salt and freshly ground
  black pepper

For the pasta dough
300g (10½oz) tipo 00 flour
3 eggs, beaten
1 tbsp water

For the filling
400g (14oz) Désirée or any
  red skin potato, peeled and
  cut into 2cm (¾in) pieces
200g (7oz) Swiss chard, stalks
  and leaves chopped
2 tbsp extra-virgin olive oil
1 small onion, finely chopped
1 tsp thyme leaves
150g (5½oz) ricotta, drained
  and squeezed of excess
  water
75g (2½oz) parmesan, grated,
  plus extra to serve
1 tsp marjoram leaves
pinch of freshly grated nutmeg

This is a classic pasta recipe from Friuli-Venezia Giulia, which is a region of Italy that is often overlooked but in my opinion is vastly underrated, as it has fantastic food and some of the best white wines of Italy. Cjarsons are a simple pansotti, or half-moon-shape pasta, and the filling can be either sweet or savoury. I have made this more of a spring-style pasta dish with the addition of peas and asparagus to serve with the potato-filled cjarsons.

Make the pasta dough. Add the flour to a large bowl, then add the eggs and water. Combine with a fork, then use your hands to form a dough. Once the dough is smooth, halve it and cover with cling film (plastic wrap). Rest in the fridge for 20 minutes.

Now make the filling. Add the potatoes to a pan of salted water, bring to the boil, cook until soft, then drain. Put through a potato ricer, season with salt and black pepper and leave to one side.

Add the chard stalks and leaves to a pan of boiling salted water, cook for 3 minutes after it comes back to the boil, then drain. Push down with some kitchen paper to remove any excess water.

Add the olive oil to a hot frying pan, then add the onion and thyme and cook over a medium heat for 5 minutes. Add the chard stalks and leaves and cook for 5 minutes until all the moisture has evaporated. Mix with the mashed potato, along with the ricotta, parmesan, marjoram and nutmeg. Check the seasoning.

Using a rolling pin, roll out each piece of pasta dough until thin enough to go through the rollers on your pasta machine. Place one end in the machine on the widest setting and roll it through. Fold the dough in half and roll again. Repeat 4 times, then roll each piece into a long sheet – when you can see the silhouette of your hand behind the pasta, it is thin enough. Cut rounds from each sheet using an 8–10cm (3¼–4in) round cutter.

Spoon 1 teaspoon of filling in the middle of each round. Brush water around the edges of the pasta, then bring the edges together to form a half-moon. Repeat with all the pasta and filling.

Add the peas, asparagus and cjarsons to a pan of boiling salted water and cook until the pasta has risen and floats for 1 minute.

Add a ladleful of the pasta cooking water with the butter to a frying pan. Using a slotted spoon, transfer the cjarsons, asparagus and peas to the frying pan and cook together for a few moments so the pasta and sauce become emulsified. Serve in warm bowls with parmesan and some black pepper.

Tomato, aubergine and potato al forno with mozzarella

Serves 8

2kg (4lb 8oz) Désirée or
  Cyprus potatoes, peeled
3 medium aubergines
  (eggplants)
600g (1lb 5oz) plum tomatoes
4 tbsp extra-virgin olive oil
8 basil leaves, torn
1 garlic clove, crushed to
  a paste with a little sea salt
2 tsp thyme leaves
100g (3½oz) breadcrumbs
100g (3½oz) grated parmesan
2 x 150g (5½oz) balls of
  mozzarella, sliced
sea salt and freshly ground
  black pepper

Thinly sliced and baked potatoes always remind me of my first job working for Max Markarian of Chez Max. It was just Max and me in the kitchen, and on a Saturday night we would do 40 covers – no small feat as the food was all made to order. I would make two potato gratins in the afternoon ready for the evening service. Spooning out the pre-cooked potatoes made my life so much easier. Think of this recipe a bit like a melanzane parmigiana, but with potatoes.

Preheat the oven to 180°C/160°C fan/350°F/Gas 4.

Using a mandoline, slice the potatoes to a 5mm (¼in) thickness and place in a bowl, covered with a damp tea (dish) towel.

Slice the aubergines into 1cm (½in) discs and mix them with a sprinkling of salt in a large bowl. Leave for 10 minutes so they release moisture, then place them in a single layer on a clean tea towel. Place another tea towel on top, then roll the aubergine slices up and push them down with all your weight so all the water is absorbed into the cloth. Keep the dried and salted aubergines to one side.

Cut the tomatoes into 1cm (½in) slices and keep to one side.

Pour 2 tablespoons of the olive oil into a large baking dish, and rub the insides so all edges are covered. Place a layer of potatoes on the bottom, then a layer of aubergines, then a layer of tomatoes. Add salt and black pepper and some basil. Repeat the layers until you have used all the potatoes, aubergines, tomatoes and basil. Cover tightly with baking paper then a layer of foil.

Bake in the oven for 45 minutes, then check the potato and aubergines are cooked by putting a sharp knife through the foil to the bottom of the roasting dish; if there is no resistance, then they are cooked. Remove the dish from the oven and remove the foil and baking paper.

Add the crushed garlic in salt, thyme, breadcrumbs, parmesan and the remaining 2 tablespoons of olive oil to a medium bowl and mix well together. Place the mozzarella slices on top of the cooked vegetables, then sprinkle over the breadcrumb and parmesan mixture.

Place back in the oven and cook for a further 20 minutes, so the breadcrumbs are a golden brown and the mozzarella has melted. Take out of the oven, place on a wire rack and leave for 10 minutes before serving.

Potatoes slow cooked with tomatoes, olives and bay leaves

Serves 6 as a side dish

2kg (4lb 8oz) Désirée or
  Cyprus potatoes, peeled
  and cut into roughly 3cm
  (1¼in) pieces
4 tbsp extra-virgin olive oil,
  plus extra to serve
2 garlic cloves, finely sliced
150g (5½oz) Italian green
  olives (nocellara are the
  best), pitted and halved
3 fresh bay leaves
600ml (20fl oz) tomato passata
  (strained tomatoes)
1 tbsp chopped flat-leaf
  parsley
sea salt and freshly ground
  black pepper

Désirée potatoes are an all-round potato – you can mash, fry, roast and bake them. In fact, most red-skinned potatoes are like this, so next time you see red potatoes, buy them. This is a very simple and delicious potato dish that is not at all complicated. Just take your time, as the more slowly it is cooked, the better it tastes.

Add the potatoes and 1 teaspoon of salt to a saucepan of water, bring to the boil, then turn down the heat and simmer for 25 minutes. Check the potatoes are cooked by pushing a sharp knife through them: if there is no resistance, then the potatoes are cooked. Drain into a colander and leave to one side.

Add the olive oil to a hot, large non-stick frying pan, add the garlic, olive halves and bay leaves and cook over a medium heat for 2 minutes, making sure you don't colour the garlic.

Add the passata and cook for 10 minutes, then add the cooked potatoes and cook slowly, turning the potatoes occasionally so they soak up all the flavour of the tomato, bay leaves and olives. Add the parsley and check the seasoning, then serve in a large, warm bowl in the middle of the table, with a drizzle of olive oil and some black pepper over the top.

Potato, onion and red pepper al forno

Serves 4

4 tbsp extra-virgin olive oil

2 red onions, finely sliced

4 red (bell) peppers, deseeded
  and cut into strips

150ml (5fl oz) red wine

600ml (20fl oz) tomato passata
  (strained tomatoes)

25g (1oz) miniature capers
  in vinegar, drained

8 basil leaves, torn

1kg (2lb 3oz) Désirée
  potatoes, peeled and
  sliced 1cm (1/2in) thick

150g (51/2oz) fontina or
  Gruyère, grated

sea salt and freshly ground
  black pepper

**Red wine with red peppers is a flavour I always associate
with my mother's cooking – the scent of the sweet peppers
cooking in red wine is a joy and the inspiration for this
recipe. The tomato and pepper mixture should be really
soft and sweet. If you can get hold of large Italian or Spanish
peppers, it will taste all the better. Try and cut them as thinly
as possible, as this will help the pepper skins break down
more quickly. The fontina crust on top is sublime.**

Add 3 tablespoons of the olive oil to a hot, large non-stick frying
pan and add the onions, red peppers and a good pinch of salt.
Cook over a medium heat for 15 minutes, with the lid on so
the peppers and onions turn soft. Remove the lid, add the red
wine and reduce for 2 minutes before adding the passata. Cook
slowly for 20 minutes so the peppers and the tomato become
sticky and sweet. Stir in the capers and basil and check the
seasoning. Remove from the heat and keep to one side.

Preheat the oven to 180°C/160°C fan/350°F/Gas 4.

Add the sliced potatoes to a large pan of boiling salted water
and cook for 2 minutes after the water has come back to the
boil, then drain and leave to steam.

Rub the insides of a baking dish with the remaining tablespoon
of olive oil. Tip in the tomato and pepper mixture, then carefully
layer the potato slices on top, so they overlap neatly. Cover
tightly with baking paper then a sheet of foil.

Cook for 25 minutes, then check the potatoes are fully cooked
by pushing a sharp knife into them; if there is no resistance, then
they are ready. Take the dish out of the oven and remove the foil
and baking paper. Scatter the grated cheese over the top and
place back in the oven on the grill (broiler) setting. Cook until the
cheese has melted, turned a golden brown and is slightly crispy.

Take the dish out of the oven, place on a wire rack and leave for
10 minutes before serving.

Pot-roasted new potatoes with garlic butter and sage

Serves 6 as a side dish

1.5kg (3lb 5oz) new potatoes,
   unpeeled, washed
5 garlic cloves, peeled
8 sage leaves
100g (3½oz) butter
½ tsp sea salt
½ lemon
freshly ground black pepper

This is one of Corinne Floris's mum's recipes. Corinne is one of my chefs in the restaurant, a very talented cook and super-organized in the kitchen. She is always making dishes on the side for the chefs and waiters after a busy service while she is preparing or even doing service. So much so that we don't even notice her making them until she presents something delicious at the end of the night – you can imagine how popular she is. Anyway, this potato dish was on the side of the stove and smelt incredible, and Corinne turned to me with a potato on a fork and said, 'This is my mother's potato recipe, what do you think?' The little potato was no looker but, wow, it tasted amazing – soft in the centre with a lovely sage butter taste. Thank you, Signora Floris.

Add all the ingredients except the lemon and black pepper to a medium saucepan and add water to cover. Place a lid on top and bring to the boil over a high heat, then turn the heat to low and leave the lid ajar.

Cook for 1 hour, or until the water has evaporated and the butter and sage are gently frying. Add a squeeze of lemon and some black pepper and serve immediately.

Index

Acknowledgements

A huge thank you to Lizzie Mayson for yet another brilliant collection of beautiful photographs – your drive and positivity keeps us all going. Abbie Fisk, it was such a pleasure to work with you. Your little laughs brought out the sunshine when we needed it (also you make the best cup of tea, ever). Louie Waller, as always brilliant prop design and so much inspiration. A massive thank you to Harriet Webster, who brings the book to life – thank you for your patience. Katherine Case, another brilliantly designed cover and book, thank you. Huge thanks to Sarah Lavelle for your support and always having something positive to say. And a massive thank you to everyone else at Quadrille who works tirelessly to make my books a success. Fiona Lindsay, big thanks for all the years we have been working together. Natalie and Lola thank you for living and eating through this book. Thanks to Steve Holmes, for your support and love of Italian food. Thank you to Patrick and Ursula Cescau for pushing me to write a book on vegetables. To my father Peter Randall, for all your input, and to my sisters Claudia and Justine, thank you. To my kitchen gang – Kane Hampshaw, Corinne Floris, Luis Diaz, Leila Faulkner, Ashna Jacob, Arezki Kareche, Robin Harriss, Aldi Mullaj, Mohammed Azard – you are all brilliant, thank you. Anamaria, Dorina, Astrid, Fernando, Francisco, Peter, Brigida, Cornelia and Sebastian – thanks for doing such a great job. Thank you to my grandson, Boaz Randall, who I can't wait to start cooking vegetables for (Max and Catalina, you are great parents and we are so proud of you). Manou, Marc, Sophie, Michael, Linda, Damiana, Barbara – thanks for always being there.

About the author

Theo Randall started working at The River Café in 1989. After a brief stint at Chez Panisse under Alice Waters, he returned to London to take up the role of Head Chef at The River Café, and remained there for 15 years. He left in 2006 to launch his first restaurant, Theo Randall at the Intercontinental, which now has a location in Hong Kong. Theo has appeared on *Saturday Kitchen* on numerous occasions, *Masterchef*, *Sunday Brunch*, *Chef's Protégé* and *My Kitchen Rules*. He also works with high-profile brands including Natoora, Coco Di Mama and Ask Italian. He has written four previous cookbooks, *Pasta*, *My Simple Italian*, *The Italian Deli Cookbook* and *Italian Pantry*.

Publishing Director: Sarah Lavelle
Commissioning Editor: Harriet Webster
Copy Editor: Sally Somers
Design Manager: Katherine Case
Photographer: Lizzie Mayson
Food Stylist: Theo Randall
Prop Stylist: Louie Waller
Head of Production: Stephen Lang
Senior Production Controller: Sabeena Atchia

Published in 2024 by Quadrille,
an imprint of Hardie Grant Publishing

Quadrille
52–54 Southwark Street
London SE1 1UN
quadrille.com

Cataloguing in Publication Data: a catalogue
record for this book is available from the
British Library.

Text © Theo Randall 2024
Design © Quadrille 2024
Photography © Lizzie Mayson 2024

ISBN 978 1 78713 992 3

Printed in China

MIX
Paper | Supporting
responsible forestry
FSC
www.fsc.org   FSC™ C020056